WILDEST OF
THE WILD WEST

View of the Las Vegas Plaza, stopping place on the Santa Fe Trail, before the arrival of the railroad in 1879. (Courtesy Museum of New Mexico, James N. Furlong photo, negative 112937)

WILDEST OF
THE WILD WEST

True Tales Of A Frontier Town
On The Santa Fe Trail

HOWARD BRYAN

*CLEAR
LIGHT PUBLISHERS*

Library of Congress Catalog Card Number: 88-71799

Printed in Spain by Novograph, S.A.

ISBN 0-940666-08-1

FRONT COVER: Unidentified rustlers of New Mexico, ca. 1878–79. (Courtesy Museum of New Mexico, negative 14262)

BACK COVER: Warning poster distributed in Las Vegas in 1882. (Courtesy Museum of New Mexico, negative 957)

*Dedicated to the memory of
J. Milnor Rudolph
1929–1986*

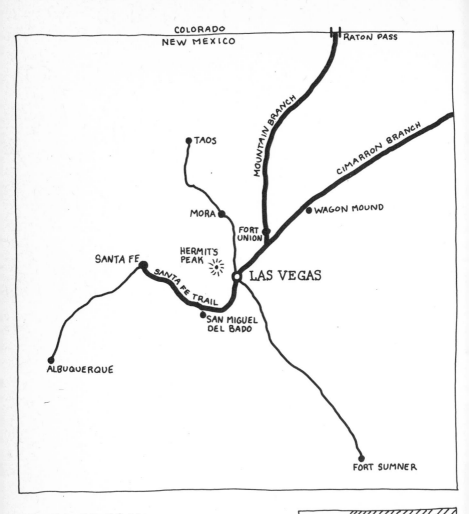

COLORADO
NEW MEXICO

RATON PASS

MOUNTAIN BRANCH

CIMARRON BRANCH

TAOS

MORA

WAGON MOUND

FORT UNION

SANTA FE

HERMIT'S PEAK

LAS VEGAS

SANTA FE TRAIL

SAN MIGUEL DEL BADO

ALBUQUERQUE

FORT SUMNER

SANTA FE TRAIL
IN NORTHEAST
NEW MEXICO

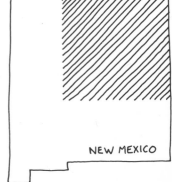

NEW MEXICO

MAP DRAWN BY LAURIE HARGETT

CONTENTS

LIST OF ILLUSTRATIONS

INTRODUCTION

By Max Evans

The story of Las Vegas, New Mexico, causes one to ponder how most historians of the West could have missed a town so wild and full of bloody bullet holes and neck-stretched hemp as to make Tombstone and Dodge City look like the headquarters for a Billy Graham Crusade. This is in no way meant to belittle the wondrous history of commerce, sheep, and cattle industries and other trade, Indian wars, and U.S. cavalry expeditions that surround the unholy action.

Howard Bryan has been researching Western history and legends of New Mexico and the Southwest in his *Albuquerque Tribune* columns since 1953. He has constantly sought the unusual, wry, and humorous elements to emphasize his knowledge and love of the West. It has never been more effective than in this book on Las Vegas, New Mexico, so properly entitled THE WILDEST OF THE WILD WEST.

The author covers the massive movement from covered

wagons to airplanes with much new historical material, and—a miracle in itself—no invented dialogue. The book ranges from stories of the first woman hanged on the Western frontier through Doc Holliday, Jesse James, Mysterious Dave Mather, and a lesser-known but probably even greater man with a crooked scheme, a nervous trigger finger, and a laugh to match it, one Hoodoo Brown. The daring and dissipated adventures of a lady known as Monte Verde is, alone, worth the price of the volume.

The newspaper dissertations from the old *Las Vegas Optic* are delights. Quoting here portions of only two: "Of late years, Gordon has been disfigured by the loss of his nose. It was bitten off by a gambler from whom he had taken money. His antagonist seized him with a grasp of iron by both ears and with his teeth wrought the disfiguration." And in a detailed description of the numerous and nefarious deeds of the aforementioned Hoodoo Brown: "A recital of the many terrible affairs with which he [Hoodoo Brown] has been connected in this country would make a whole book of horribles."

The hanging windmill on the Old Town Plaza was used so often and so publicly that its services to the community had to be voided as too great a temptation. Little boys all over town were hanging their dogs in imitation.

In 1913, Las Vegas, legitimately billed as the "Cowboy Capital of the World," almost became the capital of another kind of Western. The Lubin Film Company set up a studio there to create a make-believe cowboy capital. It worked for a while, and such widely famous actors as Tom Mix made several films there.

Howard Bryan has done those citizens of numerous countries—who are captivated by the unique, tragic, and humorous true Western history—a very big favor indeed. Make yourself comfortable and enjoy returning with Howard Bryan to a very special place and time.

Max Evans is a well-known Western author, novelist, and screenwriter whose works include "The Rounders," "The Great Wedding," "The Hi Lo Country," and "Xavier's Folly."

WILDEST OF
THE WILD WEST

Miguel A. Otero, governor of New Mexico (1897–1906), remembered Las Vegas as "the hottest town in the country" following the arrival of the railroad in 1879. (Courtesy Museum of New Mexico)

PROLOGUE

Las Vegas Optic, New Mexico
April 8, 1880

To Murderers, Confidence Men, Thieves:

The citizens of Las Vegas have tired of robbery, murder, and other crimes, that have made this town a byword in every civilized community. They have resolved to put a stop to crime, if in attaining that end they have to forget the law, and resort to a speedier justice than it will afford. All such characters are therefore, hereby notified, that they must either leave this town or conform themselves to the requirements of law, or they will be summarily dealt with. The flow of blood must and shall be stopped in this community, and the good citizens of both the old and new towns have determined to stop it, if they have to HANG by the strong arm of FORCE every violator of the law in this country.

VIGILANTES

I

They came to Las Vegas with the railroad.

Some were known as Hoodoo Brown, Mysterious Dave, Rattlesnake Sam, Dirty-Face Mike, Scar-Face Charlie, Jack-Knife Jack, Fly-Speck Sam, Hurricane Bill, Hatchet-Face Kit, Cock-Eyed Frank, Split-Nose Mike, Web-Fingered Billy, Light-Fingered Jack, Long Vest Gambler, Silent Henry, Jimmie the Duck, Hook-Nose Jim, Squint-Eyed Bob, Sawdust Charlie, Johnny Behind-the-Rocks, and Slap Jack Bill, the Pride of the Panhandle.

Others were known as Cold-Deck George, Hop-Fiend Bill, Hold-Out Jack, Six-Shooter Johnny, Black-Eyed Bruce, Short Creek Dave, Piccolo Johnny, Forty-Five Jimmie, Sheeney Frank, Double-Out Sam, Stuttering Tom, Beefsteak Mike, Pancake Billy, Dummy the Fox, Billy-Be-Damned, Caribou Brown, Hog-Foot Jim, Kickapoo George, Durango Kid, Kansas Kid, Bullshit Sam, and Handsome Harry the Dance-Hall Rustler.

Murderers, robbers, thieves, swindlers, gamblers, and just plain tramps, accompanied by the usual assortment of dance-hall girls and "soiled doves," they advanced into New Mexico as the railroad advanced, a few steps behind the construction crews and a few steps ahead of the law, lured onward by the promise of refuge, excitement, and easy money at the end of the line.

The railroad reached Las Vegas from the north and east in 1879 and then went on, building toward Santa Fe, Albuquerque, and points south, but the drifters that the railroad brought with it remained behind for a while to turn the New Mexico community into the toughest town on the Western frontier.

New Mexico historian Ralph Emerson Twitchell, in his

monumental, five-volume *The Leading Facts of New Mexican History,* wrote:

> Without exception, in the days of the construction of the Santa Fe railway into the Southwest, there was no town which harbored a more disreputable gang of gamblers, desperadoes, and outlaws than did Las Vegas. They controlled, for a while, the local peace officers, and the dance-halls and public resorts were the scenes of many shooting affrays and robberies. In the new town, in the immediate vicinity of the present Castaneda hotel, were located some of the most disreputable saloons, dance-halls, and resorts ever seen in frontier days. The gambling houses never closed and the gambling fraternity did about as they pleased. It finally became necessary to organize a committee of one hundred for the safety of the better classes and visitors to the place. Several desperadoes were summarily dealt with, taken from the jail or from their resorts and hung. Notice was served upon every "undesirable" to leave forthwith and in this manner the town was rid of as desperate a gang of cut-throats and "bad men" as ever congregated in one place in the Southwest.

Echoing Twitchell's view was Miguel A. Otero, governor of New Mexico from 1897 to 1906, and who, like Twitchell, had been an early Las Vegas resident. In his book, *My Life on the Frontier, 1864–1882,* which was first published in 1935, Otero wrote:

> For more than a year after the entry of the railroad, it can be stated without fear of contradiction that Las Vegas

*was the "hottest" town in the country. Such a statement
would be substantiated by the record, for one month, which
the old files of the (Las Vegas) Daily Optic establish. They
show that twenty-nine men were killed in and around Las
Vegas, either murdered outright or shot in self-defense or
hung by the well-regulated Vigilance Committee. Such a
record, I am certain, would be hard to parallel in the
history of any of the wild towns of the West.*

Billy the Kid, Wyatt Earp, Doc Holliday, and Jesse James are
among some of the more legendary figures of the Western
frontier who were in and out of Las Vegas when it was an
end-of-track town.

Most of the excitement, however, was provided by a
shadowy collection of reckless adventurers from various Kansas rail and cow towns who became loosely organized in Las
Vegas as the Dodge City Gang. They took over the new
railroad town of East Las Vegas, as distinguished from the
older Santa Fe Trail town of West Las Vegas on the opposite
bank of the narrow and shallow Gallinas River, and for a brief
period they ran the fledgling town pretty much as they
pleased.

Little is known about the lives of most of these frontier
ruffians, except that longevity was not one of their strong
points. Strangers, for the most part, they converged on the
new town with assumed names, aliases, and descriptive nicknames, created an atmosphere of near anarchy during their
stay, and—if they survived—melted into oblivion in the face
of mounting opposition.

Itinerant troublemakers continued to plague the frontier
town for several years following the arrival of the railroad,

prompting Las Vegas "vigilantes" to print posters in 1882 that warned:

NOTICE!
TO THIEVES, THUGS, FAKIRS AND BUNKO-STEERERS,
Among Whom Are
J.J. HARLIN, alias "OFF WHEELER;" SAW DUST
CHARLIE, WM. HEDGES, BILLY THE KID,
BILLY MULLIN, LITTLE JACK, THE
CUTER, POCK-MARKED KID, AND
ABOUT TWENTY OTHERS:
If Found within the Limits of this City
after TEN O'CLOCK P.M. this Night
you will be Invited to attend a GRAND
NECK-TIE PARTY,
The Expense of which will be borne by

100 **SUBSTANTIAL CITIZENS.**

Las Vegas, March 24th, 1882.

The Billy the Kid mentioned on the poster was counterfeiter William Wilson, and not the more notorious Billy the Kid who had been killed the year before.

A decade later, a secret crime organization composed of native-born Hispanics, described by Otero as "as tough a bunch of bad men as ever gathered outside a penal institution," unleashed more fury in and about the growing community. Led by Las Vegas tavern owner Vicente Silva, the Society of Bandits of New Mexico consisted of about forty members including three members of the local police force.

The turbulent history of Las Vegas did not begin with its role as an end-of-track town, however, for its railroad era was preceded by decades of an equally turbulent wagon road era, extending back to the period when the region was yet a part of the Republic of Mexico. Founded in 1835 as a small and isolated Mexican settlement astride the lower reaches of the Santa Fe Trail, international trade route between the United States and Mexico, Las Vegas felt the early impact of conquering armies, Indian warfare, and steady streams of immigrants from the East who spoke a different language, and who had different customs.

Unlike most of the notorious frontier towns in the American West, where the violence lasted for only brief periods, Las Vegas experienced the violent frontier with but few interruptions for more than a half-century, earning it the reputation as "the toughest town in the West" and "wildest of the Wild West." For a community that was to achieve such a wild and woolly reputation, however, Las Vegas had an inauspicious beginning that could scarcely portend the dramatic events of the future.

TRAIL TOWN TALES

Sketch of San Miguel del Bado, at the Pecos River crossing of the Santa Fe Trail, as the New Mexico community appeared in about 1848. (Courtesy Museum of New Mexico, negative 9777)

Las Vegas Grandes

Josiah Gregg, accompanying a wagon trade caravan down the Santa Fe Trail in the summer of 1831, found only a sheep camp at the site of what was to become the town of Las Vegas. In his classic book *Commerce of the Prairies,* Gregg described the scene: "At Gallinas creek, we found a large flock of sheep grazing upon the adjacent plain; while a little hovel at the foot of a cliff showed it to be a rancho. A swarthy ranchero soon made his appearance, from whom we procured a treat of goat's milk, with some dirty ewe's milk 'curdle cheese' to supply the place of bread."

Another 25 miles brought Gregg to the village of San Miguel del Bado, on the west bank of the swift-flowing Pecos River, which he said was "the first settlement of any note" he had seen on his slow journey of more than 700 miles across the plains from Independence, Missouri. Gregg wrote that San Miguel, 40 miles from trail's end at Santa Fe, consisted of "irregular clusters of mud-wall huts."

New Mexico was a part of the Republic of Mexico at the time, and the village of San Miguel, at the Pecos River ford, was considered the port of entry for the heavily laden wagons which since the early 1820s had been bearing trade goods from the United States to the New Mexico capital city of Santa Fe. Since its founding in 1794, San Miguel had served as a buffer community on the Pecos frontier between Santa Fe and nomadic Indian raiders from the plains to the east.

San Miguel consisted of a mixture of Hispanic and *genízaro* settlers, the latter being displaced Indians from various tribes who had lost their tribal identities and had become Hispanicized Roman Catholics. Most had been released after long periods of captivity by tribes other than their own.

By the 1830s, San Miguel was overpopulated, with more than 2,000 people in the vicinity, and most of the good crop and grazing lands taken. The parish priest complained to authorities of unemployment, idleness, and vagrancy in the town, and recommended that a community land grant be established beyond the confines of his parish that would benefit "industrious men and vagrant alike" and also provide a new barrier against the Indian raiders of the plains. His recommendations did not go unheeded.

In the spring of 1835, twenty-nine men of San Miguel were successful in petitioning Mexican government authorities for a grant of unoccupied land at Las Vegas Grandes, The Great Meadows, in the Gallinas River valley, a day's journey up the Santa Fe Trail toward the north and east. This land previously had been granted to Luis María Cabeza de Baca, on behalf of himself and his seventeen sons, for cultivation and pasture, but the family, after living there for some years, had been driven off by frequent Apache, Comanche, and Kiowa Indian raids.

The successful petitioners for the now unoccupied grant were Juan de Dios Maese, Miguel Archuleta, Manuel Duran, and José Antonio Casaus, on behalf of themselves and twenty-five others. They were placed in possession of their land grant, which consisted of nearly a half-million acres, during formal ceremonies on April 6, 1835.

Following instructions, they selected a townsite, chose small tracts for their homes and gardens, and began planting a few crops, mostly beans. The remainder of the large grant was designated common grazing lands for the undivided use of all those settling on the grant. The name selected for the new town was Nuestra Señora de los Dolores de Las Vegas, Our Lady of Sorrows of The Meadows.

The site was near the west bank of the Gallinas River, where the narrow stream, which rises in the lofty and pine-covered Sangre de Cristo Mountains just to the northwest, emerges from the mountain range into rolling meadow lands and begins winding in a southerly direction across the plains to empty its waters into the Pecos River. Here, at an elevation of nearly 6,500 feet, flanked by mountain peaks that rise to elevations of more than 11,000 feet, winters can be cold, snowy, and blustery, and the colonists, yet lacking suitable quarters, retreated to San Miguel for the first winter months. An initial crop failure and an Indian attack may have been factors, too.

March 5, 1836, was the date set for the colonists to reassemble at Las Vegas, but none showed up. One of them, Juan de Dios Maese, in his capacity as judge of the primary court of San Miguel del Bado, dispatched a letter on March 14 to the governor of New Mexico in Santa Fe asking for enforceable orders and regulations to compel the settlers to return and take possession of their land grant. While he had designated March 5 for them to meet at the new settlement, he told the governor, "he has not observed any of the possessors complying with my order." His letter, in translation from the original Spanish, went on to say:

> However, some of them have appeared before him with very tractable declarations in regard to their grants and in others he has observed great coolness and disregard for said land of which they are made grantees.
>
> Since these observations are so unpleasant, he appeals to your Excellency in order that you may deign to provide measures of decisions for the undersigned Judge of the Primary Court and for the grantees, in order to compel them to cultivate the lands granted to them.
>
> Your Excellency will not fail to recognize that the petitioner also is interested in his share of a tract of the land, while others with greater need to not settle it and do without it, just for personal reasons, or because they are truly afraid of being assaulted by the enemy who have heretofore attacked us, while others do not simply because of laziness.

Another difficulty, Maese wrote, was that most of the Las Vegas grantees were hoping that they would be given lands at Tecolote, midway between San Miguel and Las Vegas, adding that Tecolote "is unproductive and insufficient even for one farm, because of the scarcity of water for irrigation purposes, being suitable only for grazing purposes and to harbor the livestock of this jurisdiction and that of Las Vegas in time of threats of hostilities by the enemy." A petition for a Tecolote land grant had been turned down by the Royal Assembly the previous year, Maese wrote, while "Las Vegas was granted to all those within the jurisdiction who were destitute or in need of land for farming purposes."

Maese apparently received his enforceable orders, for by the summer of 1836 settlers were back at the Las Vegas Grant, building a town, digging irrigation ditches, and planting crops. After a shaky start, Maese had his town, a new settlement on Mexico's northeastern frontier, born two and one-quarter centuries after the founding of Santa Fe.

First Settlement of Note

Typical of New Mexico towns of the period, Las Vegas gradually took shape around a rectangular plaza, or public square, faced on the four sides by one-story, flat-roofed structures with thick walls made of adobe bricks. As the settlement grew, more structures were added along roads leading out from the central plaza. Devout Roman Catholics, the Hispanic settlers were quick to erect a small adobe church on the west side of the plaza, dedicated to Nuestra Señora de los Dolores de Las Vegas, which was to serve as the spiritual and social center of the village until it was replaced some decades later by a much larger church building a short distance west of the plaza.

The land-grant settlers could not have picked a more advantageous spot on New Mexico's northeastern frontier to build their town, for here, at the Gallinas River crossing of the Santa Fe Trail, Las Vegas replaced San Miguel del Bado as "the first settlement of any note" reached by incoming wagon trains from Missouri. The Mexican farmers and ranchers found a ready market among the weary wagoners for their fresh vegetables, fruit, grain, and meat, and the arrival of each wagon train was greeted with rejoicing and celebration. Caravans outbound for the United States also paused at Las Vegas for "last chance" supplies.

Some of the young men of the village found employment with the wagon caravans and traveled the length of the trade route as laborers and herders. Some became *ciboleros,* or buffalo hunters, riding horseback into the broad expanse of plains on periodic buffalo hunts, while a few became *comancheros,* illicit Indian traders who journeyed into the plains to rendezvous with Comanche war parties and exchange New Mexico goods for plunder seized by the Comanches during their raiding forays.

Credited with being the first United States citizen to settle permanently in Las Vegas was Levi J. Keithley, a Missourian, who arrived in 1839 and eventually became the town's first postmaster. He was followed by a few other English-speaking and French-speaking immigrants from the United States and Canada, some of whom married Hispanic women and became Mexican citizens.

Visitors to Las Vegas in 1846 described it as a primitive agricultural settlement of more than 100 dwellings, with corn-cribs and pigpens, surrounded by irrigated fields and livestock pastures.

That was the year Las Vegas felt the heel of the conqueror.

The Army of the West

As the outlying community on the Santa Fe Trail, Las Vegas was the first New Mexico town to feel the impact of the Manifest Destiny westward expansion of the United States during the Mexican War. This came about on August 14, 1846, soon after the outbreak of the war, when the trail from Missouri suddenly spawned an invasion force of some 1,500 soldiers—the United States Army of the West—which went into camp near some cornfields on the outskirts of town. The troops, preparing for battle, received word that Mexican soldiers, under the command of Gen. Manuel Armijo, governor of New Mexico, would oppose them beyond Las Vegas.

The men of Las Vegas, after concealing their women and children among some rocks and trees near the village, gathered on the plaza the next morning, August 15, to await the arrival of the U.S. commander, Gen. Stephen Watts Kearny. At 8 a.m., Gen. Kearny and members of his staff rode horseback into the crowded plaza and were met by founding father Juan de Dios Maese, the *alcalde,* or mayor, of the town.

Dismounting, Gen. Kearny suggested to Maese and two Las Vegas militia leaders that they join him in climbing to the

Gen. Stephen Watts Kearny stood on a Las Vegas rooftop in 1846 to announce that he was taking possession of New Mexico on behalf of the United States. (Courtesy Museum of New Mexico, negative 7605)

earthen roof of one of the one-story buildings facing the plaza, from which he would read a proclamation to the assembled citizens. They ascended to the roof on a crude ladder and looked down on the assembled citizens, many of them on horseback. Gen. Kearny spoke in English, his remarks translated into Spanish by an interpreter:

> *Mr. Alcalde, and people of New Mexico: I have come amongst you by the orders of my government, to take possession of your country, and extend over it the laws of the United States. We consider it, and have done so for some time, a part of the territory of the United States. We come amongst you as friends—not as enemies; as protectors—not as conquerors. We come among you for your benefit—not for your injury.*
>
> *Henceforth I absolve you from all allegiance to the Mexican government, and from all obedience to General Armijo. He is no longer your governor. I am your governor.*

This remark created quite a sensation among the listeners. When quiet was restored, Gen. Kearny continued:

> *I shall not expect you to take up arms and follow me, to fight your own people, who may oppose me; but I now tell you, that those who remain peaceably at home, attending to their crops and their herds, shall be protected by me, in their property, their persons, and their religion; and not a pepper, not an onion, shall be disturbed or taken by my troops, without pay, or by the consent of the owner. But listen! he who promises to be quiet, and is found in arms against me, I will hang!*

From the Mexican government you have never received protection. The Apaches and the Navajos come down from the mountains and carry off your sheep, and even your women, whenever they please. My government will correct all this. It will keep off the Indians, protect you in your persons and property; and, I repeat again, will protect you in your religion.

I know you are all great Catholics; that some of your priests have told you all sorts of stories—that we should ill-treat your women, and brand them on the cheek as you do your mules on the hip. It is all false. My government respects your religion as much as the Protestant religion, and allows each man to worship his Creator as his heart tells him is best. Its laws protect the Catholic as well as the Protestant; the weak as well as the strong; the poor as well as the rich. I am not a Catholic myself—I was not brought up in that faith; but, at least one-third of my army are Catholics, and I respect a good Catholic as much as a good Protestant.

There goes my army—you see but a small portion of it; there are many more behind—resistance is useless.

Mr. Alcalde, and you two captains of militia, the laws of my country require that all men who hold office under it shall take the oath of allegiance. I do not wish, for the present, until affairs become more settled, to disturb your form of government. If you are prepared to take oaths of allegiance, I shall continue you in office, and support your authority.

As Kearny began administering the oaths, he noticed that one of the militia captains had his head bowed. "Captain, look me in the face, while you repeat the oath of office," the general declared in a voice loud enough for all to hear. The brief ceremony over, Kearny descended the ladder and rejoined his troops, the army moving out toward Santa Fe and its unopposed and bloodless conquest of New Mexico under a bright sun with unfurled guidons and colors and with the sounds of bugle calls.

For forty-six-year-old Maese, as well as for many other adult citizens of Las Vegas, this was their second change of national allegiance in twenty-five years, for they were born when their land was ruled by Spain, before Mexico won its independence in 1821 to become a republic. Independence from Spain, however, had done little to change their lives.

When the conquering gringo army had departed, the Hispanic villagers returned to their homes to ponder the meaning of their new allegiance, and to wonder what the future would bring.

Rebels and Raiders

Troop movements through Las Vegas continued during the months following Gen. Kearny's arrival as additional U.S. soldiers journeyed down the wagon trail to Santa Fe to complete the conquest of Mexico's northern provinces. Col. Sterling Price, leading more than 1,000 members of the Second Regiment of Missouri Volunteers, passed through the community late in September, 1846, followed by 500 volunteers of the Mormon Battalion early in October.

Gov. Armijo had fled south from Santa Fe as Kearny's army approached the capital, and Kearny, after taking possession of the capital, organized a civil government for New Mexico, appointed civil officers, and prepared and published a set of laws for the conquered territory. He left Santa Fe on September 25 with the main body of his Army of the West and moved westward across Arizona to assist in the conquest of California.

"The people of New Mexico are now perfectly tranquil and can easily be kept so," Kearny reported to Washington the day before he left Santa Fe. "The intelligent portion know the advantages they are to derive from the change of government and express their satisfaction at it."

Events soon were to show that the general was overly optimistic in his assessment of the tranquility and satisfaction of the conquered New Mexicans.

Col. Price, who years later was to become governor of Missouri and a major general in the Confederate Army, succeeded Kearny as military commander in Santa Fe. To help secure the conquered territory and to provide better forage than was available around Santa Fe, he assigned companies of Missouri Volunteers to establish grazing camps in the vicinity of various New Mexico communities where grass was plentiful, including several on the Santa Fe Trail near Las Vegas.

In December, Price learned that Mexican loyalists in Santa Fe were plotting in secret meetings to overthrow the newly established U.S. government and to restore Mexican rule. Some of the conspirators were arrested and others fled the city, thus thwarting an open revolt that was planned in the capital on Christmas Eve, at a time when the conspirators believed Price's unruly and undisciplined volunteer soldiers would be out on the town celebrating.

Resentment against the foreign invader spread through towns and villages north of Santa Fe, however, exploding into open revolt at Taos during the early morning hours of January 19, 1847. Throngs of Taos Hispanics and Indians from nearby Taos Pueblo swept through the snowy streets before dawn, dragging Americans and American sympathizers from their homes and killing them and burning and looting their homes and businesses. Their prize victim was Taos merchant Charles Bent, whom Kearny had appointed governor of New Mexico a few months before.

The revolt spread quickly south to Mora, thirty miles north of Las Vegas, where insurgents under the leadership of Manuel Cortéz, on the morning of January 20, captured a small American wagon train as it was entering the town and executed the seven or eight Santa Fe traders accompanying it. Word of the rebellion reached Las Vegas later that day, along with a circular from rebel leaders urging the citizens "to shake off the yoke bound on us by a foreign government."

The townspeople had just assembled in Las Vegas that evening to hear the circular read when Capt. Israel R. Hendley and Lt. N.J. Williams of the Missouri Volunteers rode into town from a nearby grazing camp and learned of the rebellion that was sweeping northern New Mexico. Capt. Hendley reported that the *alcalde,* Juan de Dios Maese, declared against the insurrection at the meeting. "Early the next day I took possession of this place with a part of my command and have ordered the balance to join me today," Hendley wrote to Col. Price in Santa Fe on January 23 in what proved to be his last report.

Leading eighty men, Hendley moved north out of Las Vegas the following day and headed for Mora, camping overnight along the way and enduring a brief snowstorm. Reaching the outskirts of Mora on January 25, they found an estimated one hundred and fifty insurrectionists under arms and preparing to defend the town.

The soldiers stormed into the town, and close-range fighting raged through the streets and into the houses, until the insurgents sought refuge in a two-story fort with portholes that served the mountain valley community as a safeguard against Indian attacks. A battering ram was brought to bear against one door of the fort, and Hendley rushed into the breach to find himself in a small, smoke-filled room. A bullet fired from an adjoining room struck the captain, causing his death within a few minutes.

With the death of their captain and with no artillery to batter the strong walls of the fort, the Missouri Volunteers retreated to Las Vegas with the body of their captain, who eventually was to find a final resting place in Richmond, Missouri. The volunteers reported one of their men killed and three wounded at Mora, and said they had killed fifteen to twenty insurgents and taken fifteen prisoners.

Capt. Jesse B. Morin was sent from Santa Fe to succeed Hendley at Las Vegas. Gathering a force of about 200 men and securing one piece of artillery, he led the larger force back to Mora. The Mora insurgents fled the town when the large force approached on February 1, and the soldiers proceeded to demolish both the upper and lower plazas of the town with fire and cannon balls, leaving only a few residences standing to shelter the women and children from the cold.

Some prisoners were taken, and they were forced to lead the soldiers to the burial place of the Santa Fe traders who had been killed there January 20. Seven bodies were exhumed and carried back to Las Vegas, where they were reburied on a hill west of the plaza. They were identified as Lawrence L. Waldo, veteran trader of Westport, Missouri, and Benjamin Pruett, Romulus E. Culver, Joseph Funk, Lewis Cabanne, Mr. Noyes, and Mr. Valentine.

Three days after the destruction of Mora the revolt was crushed at Taos Pueblo, about forty-five miles north of Mora, when nearly 500 Missouri and New Mexico volunteers, commanded by Col. Price, blasted through the thick adobe walls of the mission church in which the insurgents had fortified themselves and killed about one hundred and fifty of them.

Cortéz, leader of the Mora revolt, led some of his die-hard followers to the lower reaches of the Mora River northeast of Las Vegas, joined forces with some Plains Indians, and began attacking wagon trains and U.S. grazing camps along the Santa Fe Trail in the vicinity.

Maj. Benjamin B. Edmonson of the Second Regiment of Missouri Mounted Volunteers was sent to the scene from Albuquerque, and upon his arrival at Las Vegas on May 20 was informed that marauding parties had been seen both north and south of town. He dispatched two companies of Missouri Volunteers in pursuit of these marauders, and learned that same evening that a U.S. grazing camp near the Wagon Mound, a huge, rocky formation resembling a covered wagon on the trail about forty miles northeast of Las Vegas, had been attacked by raiders who had killed one soldier, wounded two, and driven off more than 200 horses and mules.

His command reduced by two companies already in the field, Maj. Edmonson ordered in reinforcements from another grazing camp and proceeded to the Wagon Mound with from seventy-five to eighty mounted troops. Upon his arrival, he found that twelve wagons loaded with sutlers' stores also had been attacked nearby, and that the raiders, unable to gain possession of the wagons, had driven off the draft animals, sixty to seventy oxen that had been put out to graze, and killed them.

Edmonson and his men trailed the raiders about twenty miles east to the Canadian River Canyon (then known as the Red River Canyon), a deep gash in the plains. Dismounting and leading their horses down the steep and rocky walls of the canyon on the afternoon of May 26, the troopers forded the rushing river with difficulty and came under attack by from

400 to 600 men. "The hills around us were by this time literally covered with Indians and Mexicans," Edmonson reported.

Soldiers and raiders skirmished for four hours along the floor and in the jagged walls of the canyon, and at sunset the troopers made their way back up to the rim of the canyon and camped for the night. Edmonson reported that forty-one of the raiders had been killed and an unknown number wounded, and reported his own losses as one man killed and three slightly wounded.

Preparing to resume the battle the next morning, the soldiers found that the raiders had departed the canyon during the night, apparently in great haste, as they had left behind horses, cattle, and camp equipage. Edmonson and his men trailed them for miles east across the plains before losing the trail in a herd of wild horses.

Mexican farmers around Las Vegas, meanwhile, were complaining that U.S. soldiers at the grazing camps were allowing their horses, mules, and oxen to enter their corn and wheat fields and eat their crops. Their complaints were ignored.

On June 27, 1847, Mexican raiders surprised the grazing camp of Capt. Thomas M. Horine's company of mounted men near Las Vegas and drove off the horses. Lt. Robert R. Brown was sent in pursuit of the stolen horses, with Pvts. McClanahan and Quisenbury and a Mexican guide. When they did not return on schedule, it was assumed that they had been killed.

Their fate was not determined until July 5, however, when a Mexican woman visiting Las Vegas confirmed that the four had been slain and three "suspicious looking" men were apprehended by some soldiers and taken before Edmonson.

When they refused to talk, a noose was placed around the neck of one of them, and he was pulled into the air three times and almost strangled before he agreed to tell what he knew.

He said the three soldiers and their guide had trailed the stolen horses to the small settlement of Los Valles, on the Gallinas River about twelve miles south of Las Vegas, that they had met resistance in attempting to recover the horses, and that all four had been killed. Their bodies, he said, had been burned to ashes.

Edmonson left immediately for Los Valles with twenty-nine Missouri cavalrymen, followed by thirty-three infantrymen and one twelve-pound mountain howitzer. The cavalrymen, speeding ahead, reached the settlement first. Edmonson divided them into two parties, one commanded by Capt. Horine and the other by Capt. John Holloway, and ordered a charge into the village from two directions.

Villagers scattered as the cavalrymen charged into the settlement; ten of them were killed in the streets and from forty to fifty taken prisoner. A search of the houses revealed clothing, weapons, and other items belonging to the slain soldiers.

The body of Lt. Brown was found concealed among some rocks just outside the settlement. Ashes said to contain the remains of the other three were found, and the Missourians believed that the body of Lt. Brown was not burned because he wore a cross suspended from his neck.

The Missourians reduced Los Valles to ashes, leaving a few houses standing to shelter the women and children.

Believing that the Las Vegas *alcalde* was in league with the raiders, the soldiers arrested Maese and burned down his Gallinas River mill near Las Vegas. Maese later was exonerated and released. Edmonson sent forty Mexican prisoners to Santa Fe to face military court martial on charges of treason, and six of them were convicted and hanged there on August 3.

The insurgents of 1847 who were hanged at both Santa Fe and Taos considered themselves Mexican patriots rather than American traitors, and their punishment raised some eyebrows in Washington. President James Polk informed Congress, in response to questions, that while he agreed with the punishment, military officials in New Mexico were in error in "designating and describing the crimes of conquered Mexican inhabitants as treason against the United States."

What may have been the first hanging in Las Vegas occurred two years later, but it apparently had nothing to do with the Mexican revolt. Missouri newspapers carried a brief item in 1849 saying: "Robert Stanfield, who murdered Joseph Kane some three months ago at San Miguel, was hung on the 27th of July at Las Vegas." No other details were given.

The Apache Chief's Daughter

Although U.S. troops had been stationed in Las Vegas temporarily on several occasions in the late 1840s, a military post was not formally established in the town until October 2, 1849. Existing buildings in the town were rented to serve as quarters for officers and enlisted men, storehouses, stables, and corrals, at costs ranging from $260 per month in 1849 to $439 in 1851. Among the young officers stationed in Las Vegas at the time was twenty-five-year-old Lt. Ambrose E. Burnside, two years out of the U.S. Military Academy at West Point and later to become a prominent Union general during the Civil War. Most of the Missouri Volunteers had departed for home in the fall of 1847 when their enlistments expired, and were replaced for one year by Illinois Volunteers, two companies of which were assigned in and about Las Vegas in 1848 under the command of Maj. I.B. Donalson.

In 1848 Alexander Barclay, a frontier trader from England in partnership with Joseph B. Doyle, began erecting a fortified trading post known as Barclay's Fort just above the junction of the Sapello and Mora rivers, eighteen miles northeast of Las Vegas. A high wall surrounded a rectangular complex of adobe buildings and stables, one acre in extent, and at each of the two corners was a round tower equipped with a small cannon.

It was an ideal location for trade, for here converged the two main branches of the Santa Fe Trail that had parted in Kansas—the Mountain Branch from the north and the Cimarron Cutoff from the northeast—now joining to form a single track through Las Vegas and on to Santa Fe. Barclay's Fort became a popular supply point and resting place for trail travelers and soldiers, but it was a private enterprise never garrisoned by U.S. troops.

Establishment of the Las Vegas military post coincided with renewed violence on the Santa Fe Trail, as Jicarilla Apache and Ute Indians began attacking trail travelers with increased fury. The reason for this outbreak of hostilities was told several years later by Francisco Chacón, a Jicarilla Apache chief, during 1852 conferences with government officials at Abiquiu, north of Santa Fe. According to the *Santa Fe Gazette,* the newspaper that published his account on November 27, 1852, Chacón was usually reliable.

Chacón said he had taken his people to Las Vegas to make peace in the late summer of 1849, only to be attacked by an armed party that killed fourteen of the Indians. He said that a young woman, the daughter of Chief Lobo Blanco (White Wolf), was captured during the attack and lodged in jail at Las Vegas.

Chacón was referring to a skirmish between U.S. troops and Jicarilla Apaches that had occurred on the outskirts of Las Vegas on August 16, 1849. The military version of the affair, as reported by Capt. H.R. Judd to his superiors, was published in several frontier newspapers at the time:

Las Vegas, August 16.

Sir: I have the honor to report that a party numbering about 40 of Apaches came to this post today with an evident design of committing depredations should a chance be presented, as well as to supply themselves with what powder and lead they could obtain by barter or otherwise. Many of them were recognized as being the same Indians who so often falsely treated for peace at Taos, and this band undoubtedly was engaged in the many murders and robberies committed during the past year along this frontier.

I, therefore, determined to seize this party, having made no professions of friendship to them; and for this purpose ordered a command under Lieut. Burnside to proceed to their camp, about a half a mile from this place. The Indians were already in the saddle and prepared for any emergency which might arise after receiving from me an abrupt dismissal.

Lieut. Burnside advancing within short range of their arrows, halted his party in the hope of recalling the Indians, who, turning their horses, delivered a flight of arrows and fled with speed over the rough hills and ravines beyond Las Vegas.

A charge of skirmishers was immediately ordered by the Lieutenant, who led his men against the flying but boldly resisting enemy. It is unnecessary to mention the details of an affair which was a hand-to-hand conflict, the sabre being the only weapon used with advantage by our people. Out of this band it is supposed that but eight or ten warriors escaped; six prisoners and three bodies have been brought in, and many of the dead remain in the ravines where they were sabred.

Gen. Ambrose E. Burnside of Civil War fame fought Apaches at Las Vegas as a young lieutenant. (Courtesy Andy Gregg)

Thirteen animals, with their rude equipments, also have been secured. The pursuit was followed some 9 miles, over a country almost impassable under less exciting circumstances.

Lieut. Burnside was wounded (slightly) by an arrow just below the ear; Lance-Sergeant Ambrose severely, by an arrow passing completely through his left forearm, and Pvt. Meader received a painful contusion below the eye, from the end of a lance.

It was during this running battle that the daughter of Chief Lobo Blanco was captured.

Chief Chacón, at the 1852 Abiquiu conference, told the Santa Fe newspaper that a group of U.S. soldiers took the young woman from the Las Vegas jail one day and conducted her up the trail to the Wagon Mound, the towering Santa Fe Trail natural landmark, and demanded that she point out to them the location of the Jicarilla Apache camp.

"A few men went with her to the top of the mound, where she seized a knife and attacked them, making so desperate a fight that they were obliged to shoot her," the Santa Fe newspaper article said.

New Mexico Indian Agent John Greiner gave a slightly different version of the dramatic episode. Greiner reported that twenty soldiers from Las Vegas, under the command of Sgt. Henry Swartwond, went in pursuit of some Indians and took the Apache chief's daughter along as a guide, and also as a hostage to be exchanged for a white woman captured by the Apaches. The detachment camped for the night at the Wagon Mound, he said, and the young Indian woman asked to go to the top of the mound. Reaching the top, she began to weep, causing the soldiers to believe that she could see some sign of her people and was trying to warn them.

In the morning, as the soldiers were trying to load the woman into a wagon at the foot of the mound, she seized a butcher knife and tried to stab them. They began chasing her around the campfire, between the mules and the wagons, and in her frenzy she began stabbing the mules, one of which died shortly thereafter.

A Sgt. Martinez then shot her in the head, the report said—an act for which her father would take revenge later—and the soldiers returned to Las Vegas. Chacón said that Chino, another Apache chief, retaliated by attacking a small party near the Wagon Mound and taking some captives, but that Chino was killed in this engagement.

Kit Carson to the Rescue

The Las Vegas post had been established for less than a month when the first news was received of a Santa Fe Trail tragedy that was to shock the entire Southwestern frontier. Charles L. Spencer, a Santa Fe merchant, brought the news to the post on October 27, 1849.

Spencer said that he and three others, while returning to New Mexico from the east in two horse-drawn carriages, had come upon a grisly sight on the night of October 25 as they approached the Point of Rocks, a natural landmark on the Cimarron branch of the trail about 100 miles northeast of Las Vegas. By the light of the moon they saw an overturned coach, with its contents scattered about, and the bodies of six or seven men lying on the ground nearby, victims of an Indian attack.

Spencer and his companions, Alexander Barclay, George Simpson, and Isaac Adamson, paused only briefly to investigate the scene, fearing that Indians were still in the vicinity, and sped on down the trail to Barclay's Fort, from which Spencer went on to Las Vegas, saying he had gone seventy-eight hours without rest. Brevet Capt. Henry R. Judd, U.S. Third Artillery, the commanding officer at the post, relayed

35

the news by express messenger to military headquarters in Santa Fe.

More details were learned a day or so later with the arrival in Las Vegas of a Santa Fe-bound wagon caravan led by Francis X. Aubry. The colorful and dashing French-Canadian freighter, trader, and trail blazer had earned the nickname "Telegraph Aubry" the previous year by using relays of horses to race from Santa Fe to Independence, a distance of 780 miles, in the record time of five days and sixteen hours.

From Aubry it was learned that one of the victims was James M. White, a prominent and popular Santa Fe merchant, and that his wife, Ann Dunn White, and small daughter, Virginia, had been captured and carried off by the Jicarilla Apaches. White, formerly of Virginia, had opened his Santa Fe store in August, 1848, and a year later had gone east to get his wife and child and take them to Santa Fe. With his family, a black female servant, and thirteen wagonloads of merchandise, White embarked down the Santa Fe Trail from Missouri on September 15, 1849, joining the large Aubry caravan.

The caravan reached Cold Spring (now in the Oklahoma Panhandle) on October 23. As cold weather was setting in and it was felt that any danger of Indian attack had passed, White decided to leave his wagons with the caravan and hurry on to Santa Fe in his carriage with his wife, child, and servant girl. They were joined by William Callaway, an Aubry wagon master; Ben Bushman, a mulatto from St. Louis; two Germans from St. Louis; and a Mexican.

While camped at a spring east of Point of Rocks, apparently on the morning of October 25, the White party was approached by some Apache Indians who demanded presents. The Indians were ordered out of the camp, whereupon an estimated 100 Apaches, led by Lobo Blanco (White Wolf), attacked the camp, killed all the men, and captured Mrs. White, her daughter, and the servant girl. Before leaving the vicinity the Apaches opened fire on a small party of Mexican *ciboleros* (buffalo hunters) that was proceeding along the trail near Point of Rocks, and killed several of them.

The bodies of the dead were buried a day or so later when the Aubry caravan reached the disaster scene. Following his arrival in Santa Fe, Aubry and other private citizens offered rewards totaling more than $1,000 for the recovery of Mrs. White and her daughter.

From Taos, a company of First U.S. Dragoons, commanded by Maj. William N. Grier, was ordered east in pursuit of the Apaches. The soldiers crossed over the Sangre de Cristo Mountains to the settlement of Rayado, where frontiersman Kit Carson joined the command as a scout. They continued eastward to the massacre site, identified as Rock Spring, 10 miles east of Point of Rocks and about 100 miles from Taos. The site was littered with broken trunks, smashed objects, and pieces of harness.

For the next ten or twelve days, the soldiers followed the trail of the Apaches through occasional snow south to the Canadian River and then east along that stream to near the Texas border where the Apache camp was found on November 17. Carson, first to spot the camp, saw that the Apaches were unaware of the approach of the dragoons. He began to charge toward the camp, shouting for the dragoons to follow him.

Maj. Grier hesitated, however, hoping to parley with the Indians, which gave the Apaches an opportunity to grab their weapons and begin firing at the soldiers. One rifle ball, fired

Christopher "Kit" Carson joined the search for the woman and her child captured by Apaches on the Santa Fe Trail. (Courtesy Museum of New Mexico, negative 13307)

at long range, pierced Grier's heavy coat and buried itself in the thick gauntlets which were folded beneath his coat, causing him to suffer only a stomach bruise.

The Apaches fled the camp, leaving most of their belongings behind, and in the skirmishing that followed, one or two were killed and several taken prisoner. The lifeless body of Mrs. White was found sitting against a willow tree, her still warm body pierced with arrows. No trace was found of her daughter or of the servant girl. Near Mrs. White's body, Carson picked up a small book she had been carrying and learned to his surprise that it was a recently published novel about him that made him out to be a great hero—the first of its kind he had seen. He could not read it, however, as he had spent most of his life on the frontier and was illiterate.

On the return trek to Taos, the soldiers were engulfed by a blizzard which Carson said was the fiercest he had ever seen, and the command sought refuge in some tall timber near Las Vegas, where one dragoon froze to death. It was learned that some of the Apaches, who had lost clothing and blankets in the attack on their camp, perished in the same storm. When the storm had abated, Grier's command found warmth in Las Vegas, where they were greeted at the military post by Capt. Judd.

Periodic reports and rumors that the White child had been seen from time to time among the Apaches prompted Congress in 1850 to appropriate $1,500 to be paid as a reward or ransom for her delivery. The child was never found, however, and the money never collected. Chacón, at the 1852 Abiquiu conference, denied any knowledge of the fate of the child.

In the 1920s, more than seventy years after the child's

capture, some U.S. Indian Service officials became convinced that an elderly woman of the Jicarilla Apache Tribe at Dulce, on the reservation in northern New Mexico, was the long lost White girl. An informal and unpublicized investigation into the background of Mrs. Marguerita Inez, apparently of Anglo Saxon descent, produced inconclusive results.

One of the government officials, Chester E. Faris, questioned elderly tribal members about the identity of the woman, but the answer in each case was a blank stare. Finally, he approached the oldest member of the tribe and asked him point-blank about the woman's background.

"If we told you about that," the Indian replied, "you would kill us yet."

Through various hints and bits of information gathered in succeeding years, the officials became satisfied in their own minds that Mrs. Inez was indeed the long missing captive. On one occasion, in fact, a physician named White who was related to the ill-fated family was introduced to Mrs. Inez after being told that she was his long lost relative. The elderly woman herself was not questioned about her background. If she knew of her origin, she apparently said nothing about it.

Death at the Wagon Mound

Chief Lobo Blanco, who led the attacks on the White party and the *ciboleros* in 1849, struck at the Santa Fe Trail again in the spring of 1850 at the very place where his daughter had been killed the year before. A party of Santa Fe traders that passed north through Las Vegas in May 1850 hurried back to town a short while later with reports of a shocking discovery on the trail at the foot of the Wagon Mound. They told of finding the bodies of at least ten men in and about a U.S. mail wagon, and said the ground around the wagon was littered with dead horses and mules, Indian arrows, and pieces of mail from mail sacks that had been ripped open. They brought with them some of the mail they had gathered at the scene as proof of their find.

Brevet Lt. Col. Edmund B. Alexander, U.S. Third Infantry, who on April 23 had succeeded Capt. Henry R. Judd as commander of the Las Vegas military post, sent a detachment of mounted artillerymen to the scene on May 21 under the command of Lt. Ambrose E. Burnside, U.S. Third Artillery. Lt. Burnside took along Alexander Barclay, whom he said "has been in the country for many years and knows the Indian habits perfectly."

The soldiers found the wagon the next day about a half-mile from the foot of the Wagon Mound, and Burnside recognized it at once as one which the mail carriers James Clay and Frank Hendrickson used to transport mail between Santa Fe and Fort Leavenworth, Kansas.

The mail wagon had passed through Las Vegas about two months before on its way to Fort Leavenworth, and was returning to Santa Fe when it was attacked. The bodies of two men were found in the wagon, and the bodies of eight other men were found nearby. Barclay picked some of the arrows off the ground and examined them. "Jicarilla Apache and Ute," he said.

The spot where the ill-fated party had camped was found about a mile up the trail, indicating that the Indians had attacked early in the morning, shortly after the group had got under way. Three of the bodies were identified as mail carriers, the remainder as members of another party that had joined them along the way.

Lt. Burnside, after conducting an investigation at the scene, came to a number of conclusions, which he listed in his official report. These included:

> *That the mail party with five or six other persons that joined it arrived at the Wagon Mound either before the snow fell on the third of this month (May) or whilst the snow was still on the ground, for no tracks of any description could be seen.*
>
> *That the wagon with eight of the party started from camp, two of the party (not mail carriers) mounted on American horses remained at the fire for a short time;*
>
> *Afterwards, starting, were charged upon by the Indi-*

ans, who were laying behind the small mound at the foot of the Wagon Mound, their horses killed and them wounded, they ran to the wagon and were assisted in by the main party;

While in the act of doing this, the party were charged upon by the Indians, thrown into a state of confusion, and finally all killed within 75 yards of the wagon, on either side of the road.

The officer added that the two men found in the wagon were wounded in their left thighs—"the most common wound a man receives on horseback and one which could not have been inflicted in the wagon."

The large number of arrows found on the ground indicated that the attacking party was a large one, he continued, adding that the best evidence of this was the small space in which the entire party had been killed. He estimated that at least 100 warriors participated in the attack. Burnside said that so large a party of Americans had never before been entirely destroyed by Indians in that portion of the territory, and that in fact ten Americans had always been considered comparatively safe traveling in that part of the Santa Fe Trail with proper care.

"The bodies were buried in a common grave," he reported, "and the wagon with all the rubbish were burned over it to prevent, if possible, the bodies being dug up by wolves."

The slain mail carriers, in addition to Clay and Hendrickson, included Thomas E. Branton, recently arrived on the frontier from his home in Middletown, Connecticut. The other victims, who had joined the mail wagon along the trail, were identified as Thomas W. Flournoy, Moses Goldstein,

Early view of the Wagon Mound, natural landmark on the Santa Fe Trail, with unidentified horsemen in foreground. (Courtesy Museum of New Mexico, F.E. Evans photo, negative 122156)

Benjamin Shaw, John Duty, John Freeman, John Williams, and a German teamster.

Death at the Wagon Mound ended a series of trials and tribulations for Goldstein, a veteran Santa Fe trader who had just spent the winter with a stranded wagon train in Kansas. While traveling from Santa Fe to Independence the previous September, Goldstein and two companions had been captured by about forty Arapaho and Apache Indians on the trail east of Rabbit Ear Creek in northeast New Mexico and robbed of their possessions, Goldstein losing about $600. The Indians, after debating the fate of their three victims, gave them some mules and allowed them to proceed.

Goldstein had begun his return trip to Santa Fe from Independence on about October 1 with a twenty-wagon train that on November 17 was caught in a severe, three-day snowstorm during which all the oxen died. The train was stranded thirty or forty miles south of the Arkansas River in Kansas, on the prairie at least thirty miles from the nearest timber. Goldstein and about seven other men, who remained with the stranded wagons for the remainder of the winter, were forced to burn two of the wagons to keep warm during extreme cold spells.

In the spring, a relief train headed by Thomas Flournoy was sent from Missouri to the rescue with fresh draft animals. Upon its arrival, Goldstein decided to join Flournoy and other members of the relief party in riding horseback on to Santa Fe. The party joined the ill-fated mail wagon along the way, and all perished at the Wagon Mound.

Years earlier, in July 1846, one of Goldstein's wagons on the trail had been closed down by military authorities who accused him of selling whisky to soldiers at "exhorbitant

45

prices," $1 per pint for 18-cent whisky, and 50 cents a drink.

The attack on the mail wagon was recalled several years later by Francisco Chacón, the Jicarilla Apache chief. Quoted by the *Santa Fe Gazette* in 1852, he said that five Apaches and four Utes were killed in the fight and were buried behind the Wagon Mound near a small lake. An unidentified Apache chief—possibly Chacón—said in Santa Fe that the Jicarillas had opened the attack on the wagon one morning and had fought all day, during which two of the Americans were wounded. He said they were joined that night by a party of Ute Indians who told the Apaches that they "did not know how to fight Americans" and that they would show them how. The combined forces resumed the attack the next day.

When the U.S. Post Office Department inaugurated monthly mail service between Independence, Missouri, and Santa Fe on July 1, 1850, the mail contractors, Waldo, Hall and Co., took every precaution to prevent a calamity such as the one that had befallen the mail wagon less than two months before. A description of the mail coaches and armed guards was published in the Missouri Commonwealth at Independence, which said in part:

> *The stages are got up in splendid style, and each are capable of conveying eight passengers. The bodies are beautifully painted, and made water-tight, with a view of using them as boats in ferrying streams. The team consists of six mules to each coach.*
>
> *The mail is guarded by eight men, armed as follows: Each man has at his side, strapped up in the stage, one of Colt's revolving rifles; in a holster, below, one of Colt's long*

revolving pistols, and in his belt a small Colt revolver,
besides a hunting knife; so that these eight men are pre-
pared, in case of attack, to discharge one hundred and
thirty-six shots without stopping to load! This is equal to
a small army, armed as in olden times, and from the
courageous appearance of this escort, prepared as they are,
either for offensive or defensive warfare with the savages, we
have no apprehensions for the safety of the mails.

The Las Vegas military post ceased to exist following the establishment in 1851 of Fort Union. On the Santa Fe Trail about twenty-five miles northeast of town, it was a fort destined to become the largest U.S. military installation in the Southwest. The most distinguished alumnus of the short-lived Las Vegas military post was Lt. Burnside, who went on to become a major general in the Union Army during the Civil War, governor of Rhode Island, and a U.S. senator from that state. His unusual style of facial hair became known as "burnsides," the word later transposed to "sideburns."

Lobo Blanco, who had achieved revenge for the death of his daughter, met his own death in the spring of 1854 during a skirmish with U.S. troops near the Canadian River on New Mexico's eastern plains. In February of that year, the Jicarilla Apaches were believed responsible for the theft of some cattle belonging to Samuel Watrous, beef contractor for Fort Union. Lt. David Bell was sent east from the fort with a detachment of Second Dragoons in an effort to find the thieves and recover the livestock.

Early in March, Lt. Bell and his men encountered Lobo Blanco and his Apaches on the plains, and during a tense parley with them, the Apaches denied stealing the cattle and blamed the theft on the Utes. When Bell answered that he would hold Lobo Blanco until the cattle thieves were produced, the chief resisted and a skirmish ensued during which two soldiers and five Apaches, including Lobo Blanco, were killed.

According to an early popular version of the encounter, Bell and the Apache chief agreed to fight a duel in an open area between the dragoon and Apache lines. Lobo Blanco, who was standing, suddenly dropped to one knee and fired at Bell, who was on his horse. The lieutenant threw his body forward, causing his horse to rear, and fired several bullets into the chief. Lobo Blanco did not expire until soldiers smashed his head with a large rock.

The Pettifogger

A so-called "American colony" was established in Las Vegas in the 1850s when a few English-speaking immigrants from the East established homes and businesses in the Hispanic farm and ranch community. The newcomers considered the village rather primitive and unattractive, consisting of one-story houses of mud (adobe bricks) scattered around a plaza that was alternately dusty in dry weather and muddy in wet weather. Nevertheless, they saw economic opportunities in the town due to its strategic location on the Santa Fe Trail and its being the nearest town to the newly established Fort Union.

Also luring the new settlers was the fact that New Mexico no longer was a foreign country. In 1850, Congress had divided the conquered Mexican regions into the Territory of New Mexico, which also included Arizona, and the State of California. County lines were drawn in the new territory in 1852, placing Las Vegas in San Miguel County with the county seat at San Miguel del Bado on the Rio Pecos.

The new military post and increasing traffic on the Santa Fe Trail created a growing demand for goods and services that the newcomers were eager to meet. For weary travelers,

Henry Connelly and E.F. Mitchell erected a hotel on the southeast corner of the plaza, complete with stables and corrals and a bar and recreation room called Buffalo Hall, eventually to become known as "the poker capital of New Mexico."

Dr. J.M. Whitlock, first physician to practice in Las Vegas, joined in a partnership to erect a sawmill north of town, the first of its kind in the region. Michael Des Marais, a French-Canadian, built a flour mill. Other new settlers, such as F.O. Kihlberg, the Kitchen brothers, and the Dold brothers, operated mercantile, trade, and stock-raising enterprises.

For years to come, the Spanish-speaking and English-speaking neighbors were designated and commonly referred to as "Mexicans" and "Americans," respectively—inaccurately, of course, since all were Americans, and the region no longer was a part of Mexico. Some of the newcomers married Hispanic women, and some took Hispanic women as common-law wives. Although prejudices existed on each side, the two ethnic groups in Las Vegas lived in relative harmony, and major problems and acts of violence in the following years usually were intra-ethnic rather than inter-ethnic—Mexican versus Mexican and American versus American.

An example of this was revealed years later by one of the early newcomers, Arthur L. Morrison, who had accompanied a wagon caravan to New Mexico in 1849 and had settled in Las Vegas to open a sutler store. In an interview published in the *Las Vegas Optic* on October 30, 1895, Morrison told of a young Chicago lawyer who arrived in Las Vegas on a wagon train in the early 1850s, decided that the town needed a lawyer, and set up practice in a small adobe building just off the plaza. His name, Morrison said, was Joseph E. Gary. He became popular among the Hispanics of the village, who called him Don José, and within a year or so they elected him *alcalde,* or mayor, of the town.

Gary was less popular among members of the American colony, however, who referred to him derisively as "the pettifogger"—which can be roughly defined as a shyster. Deciding one November day in 1854 or 1855 that the pettifogger must go, these citizens met to lay plans as to how the task would be accomplished. It was decided that Dr. Whitlock would provoke an argument with the lawyer and challenge him to a duel. The challenge, they believed, would be enough to scare Gary out of town.

Dr. Whitlock, in accordance with the plan, challenged the lawyer to a duel, and to the amazement of all concerned, Gary accepted the challenge. Gary chose Jim Barrett as his second, and Dr. Whitlock chose Morrison.

At 3 o'clock that afternoon, all repaired to a grassy spot on the banks of the Gallinas a short distance above town. Gary, attired in a dark suit of clothing, appeared a little nervous and pale, but was cool. Dr. Whitlock wore a dark suit of clothes which exposed a large expanse of shirt front. "If I am hit, I want to be hit in the heart, and not be crippled for life," the physician explained.

The seconds loaded the two pistols, described by Morrison as "old Navy pattern and very large," and it was decided that the two men would fire at the count of "three" from a distance of fifteen paces. After the two men had taken their positions, Morrison counted to three. The two fired at one another simultaneously. Dr. Whitlock staggered, threw his left hand over his heart, and exclaimed, "I am killed." He sank to the ground, a large red patch appearing on his shirt front.

Gary left for home immediately, accompanied by his second, who advised him to leave town before Dr. Whitlock's friends found and hanged him. The lawyer packed his possessions in a wagon and headed out of Las Vegas that night. Morrison said that Gary did not learn until twenty-five years later that the Las Vegas duel actually was a sham battle, that both guns had been loaded with blanks, and that the "blood" he saw on Dr. Whitlock's shirt was red paint which the physician had concealed in his left hand.

Morrison said in the 1895 newspaper interview that the young lawyer later made a fortune and became a nationally prominent judge in Chicago in the 1880s, but in this he apparently was in error, for the famous Chicago judge of the 1880s was Elbert Henry Gary. This Gary, born in 1846, was a founder of the U.S. Steel Corporation and the man for whom Gary, Indiana, was named. Dr. Whitlock, meanwhile, left his Las Vegas practice and business enterprises in 1861 to join the First Infantry, New Mexico Volunteers, as regimental surgeon, serving under his close friend, Col. Christopher "Kit" Carson. He was discharged in 1862.

In November 1862, while visiting Col. Carson at Fort Stanton, about 200 miles south of Las Vegas, Dr. Whitlock became engaged in a personal altercation with Capt. James "Paddy" Graydon, a colorful and controversial cavalryman with the First Regiment, New Mexico Volunteers. Dr. Whitlock accused Capt. Graydon and his men of needlessly attacking a peaceful Mescalero Apache camp in the mountains nearby and killing a chief and nine warriors, calling this a "treacherous assassination," and the company commander "a murderer and a thief."

The two antagonists exchanged angry words and angry notes, and on the morning of November 5, in the presence of

Col. Carson on the parade ground, the two drew their pistols and began firing at one another. Capt. Graydon, shot in the breast, fell to the ground, exclaiming, "The damned rascal has killed me."

Graydon's soldiers, attracted to the scene by the shots and finding their popular commander dying, pursued Dr. Whitlock to the sutler store. Dr. Whitlock sought refuge inside the store, and when the soldiers began shooting at the doors and windows of the store, he tried to escape out a door. The soldiers shot him down in his tracks, his body riddled with bullets and buckshot.

An angry Carson, the post commander, ordered the immediate arrests of the ringleaders, who were sent off to a Santa Fe jail from which they later escaped. Graydon died four days after the encounter. Both Graydon and Whitlock lie buried today in the National Cemetery at Santa Fe.

Judge Kirby Benedict, friend of Abraham Lincoln, sentenced a Las Vegas woman to be hanged for murder and to pay the costs of her execution. (Courtesy Museum of New Mexico, negative 6997)

The Hanging of Paula Angel

As chief justice of the New Mexico Supreme Court during the Civil War era, Kirby Benedict was required to hold court in each of New Mexico's nine counties twice each year. From his home in Santa Fe, Judge Benedict, accompanied by an entourage of lawyers and court officials, traveled on horseback or in horse-drawn vehicles to all parts of the vast territory, pausing in principal communities to hold sessions of District Court. During their twice-yearly visits to Las Vegas, the judge, lawyers, and court officials often spent their evenings drinking and playing poker at the Exchange Hotel's Buffalo Hall on the southeast corner of the plaza.

One one of these occasions, an observer who noted that some of the court officials engaged in illegal gambling at the hotel took the information to the grand jury, then in session, giving the names of those involved. In court the next morning, the names of those indicted on charges of illegal gambling were called out, and one by one, the surprised lawyers stood up and entered guilty pleas. Each paid a fine. When Benedict's name was called, the judge stood up and said, "Kirby Benedict enters a plea of guilty, and the court assesses his fine at $10 and costs, and what is more, Kirby Benedict will pay it."

During the March term of court at Las Vegas in 1861 the controversial judge also presided over the trial of a woman charged with murder and upon her conviction sentenced her to death by hanging. The few newspapers in New Mexico at the time made no mention of the trial or the hanging, and it was well into the twentieth century before some researchers were able to piece the story together from what they said were some old Spanish-language court documents and eye-witness stories handed down through several generations.

Most modern accounts identify the condemned Hispanic woman as Paula Angel, although her name also has been given as Pablita Martín and Pablita Sandoval. No hint is given of her age or marital status. There is some evidence that she lived along the Sapello River about a dozen miles north of Las Vegas.

Paula Angel was tried before a jury of twelve men upon an indictment charging her with murdering Juan Miguel Martín, who was said to have been her lover. He had broken off his romance with her, the story goes, and she had asked him for a final meeting. During a farewell embrace, she stabbed him to death with a knife she had concealed under her shawl.

The jury found her guilty of murder in the first degree, and on March 28, 1861, Judge Benedict sentenced her to be "hanged by the neck until dead on Friday, April 26, 1861, between the hours of 10 o'clock in the forenoon and 4 o'clock in the afternoon." In addition, it is said, the judge ordered the woman to pay the entire costs of the action, up to and including the hanging.

Antonio Abad Herrera, sheriff of San Miguel County,

was ordered to take the condemned woman to a suitable place within the Town of Las Vegas and within one mile of the church, and carry out the sentence. Paula's attorney, Spruce M. Baird, asked permission to appeal the verdict, and Judge Benedict granted the appeal but ordered that the appeal should "in no manner operate as a stay of execution." Sheriff Herrera apparently relished the idea of hanging Paula Angel. It is said he taunted and tormented his prisoner during the month between her conviction and the date of her execution, reminding her each day that she had one less day to live.

A large crowd, consisting of spectators from miles around, gathered in a cottonwood grove at the northwest edge of town on April 26 to witness the hanging of Paula Angel. Sheriff Herrera arrived on the scene driving a wagon; his prisoner, pale and trembling, was seated on her coffin in the back. The sheriff halted the wagon directly beneath a hangman's noose that was dangling from the limb of one of the large cottonwood trees.

As the crowd watched silently, the sheriff stood Paula in the wagon bed, placed the noose around her neck, and whipped the wagon team away, leaving her hanging in midair. The sheriff had neglected to tie her arms, however, and she grabbed the rope above her head and tried frantically to pull herself upwards from the strangling noose. Horrified, the sheriff ran to the dangling woman, grabbed her around her waist, and tried to pull her downwards to her death. The crowd rushed in, pushed the sheriff away, and cut the gasping woman down, protesting that she had been hanged and that the sentence of the court had been carried out.

During the shouting and confusion, José D. Sena, a prominent Santa Fe citizen, climbed up on the wagon, calmed the crowd, and read to them the warrant of execution, stressing that it stated the woman was to be hanged by the neck "until dead," by 4 o'clock that day, that she was not dead, and that it was not yet 4 o'clock. Once again, Paula Angel was placed in the wagon, this time with her arms bound. The wagon was driven from beneath her, and she paid the supreme penalty— the first woman to be hanged on the Western frontier.

Five years later, Judge Benedict was removed from the bench by President Andrew Johnson because of growing reports of his heavy drinking and carousing, thus bringing to an end an otherwise distinguished judicial career. Born in Connecticut in 1810, Benedict had left home at an early age, had lived on an Ohio farm for a while, and had studied law with a prominent attorney at Natchez, Mississippi. As a lawyer in Illinois, he rode circuit for sixteen years with fellow lawyers Abraham Lincoln and Stephen A. Douglas. President Franklin Pierce appointed him to the bench in New Mexico in 1853.

During the Civil War, some prominent Santa Fe citizens wrote to President Lincoln urging him to remove Benedict as chief justice of the New Mexico Supreme Court and replace him with "a good sober man." They complained that the judge frequented saloons and gambling halls and was often seen drunk and reeling around the streets. President Lincoln's reply was short and to the point: "Well, gentlemen, I know Benedict. We have been friends for over 30 years. He may imbibe to excess, but Benedict drunk knows more law than all the others on the bench in New Mexico know sober. I shall not disturb him."

In 1866, President Andrew Johnson, bowing to increased pressure from New Mexico, removed Benedict from the bench. The judge, considered a distinguished jurist with a sharp legal mind regardless of his other difficulties, died debt-ridden in Santa Fe in 1874.

Judge Benedict is best remembered for the wording of a death sentence he pronounced upon Jesús María Martínez during a court session at Taos in April 1864. A Taos jury convicted Martínez of murder in the death of Julián Trujillo, a blacksmith—a murder described by *The New Mexican* at Santa Fe as "revengeful, vindictive and wanton." This, according to one of the lawyers who was present, is how Benedict sentenced the young man:

> *Jesús María Martínez, stand up!*
>
> *Jesús María Martínez, you have been indicted, tried and convicted by a jury of your countrymen of the crime of murder, and the court is now about to pass upon you the dread sentence of the law.*
>
> *As a usual thing, Jesús María Martínez, it is a painful duty for the judge of a court to pronounce upon a human being the sentence of death. There is something horrible about it, and the mind of the court naturally revolts from the performance of such a duty. Happily, however, your case is relieved of all such unpleasant features, and the court takes positive delight in sentencing you to death.*
>
> *You are a young man, Jesús María Martínez, apparently of good physical condition and robust health. Ordinarily you might have looked forward to many years of life, and the court has no doubt you have, and have expected to die at a ripe old age, but you are about to be cut off in consequence of your own act.*
>
> *Jesús María Martínez, it is now springtime. In a little*

while the grass will be springing up green in these beautiful valleys, and on these broad mesas and mountainsides flowers will be blooming, birds will be singing their sweet carols, and nature will be putting on her most gorgeous and her most attractive robes, and life will be pleasant and men will want to stay; but none of this for you, Jesús María Martínez.

The flowers will not bloom for you, Jesús María Martínez; the birds will not carol for you, Jesús María Martínez. When these things come to gladden the senses of men, you will be occupying a space about six by two beneath the sod, and the green grass and those beautiful flowers will be growing over your lowly head.

The sentence of the court is that you be taken from this place to the county jail, and that you be kept there safely and securely confined, in the custody of the sheriff, until the day appointed for your execution.

(Be very careful, Mr. Sheriff, that he have no opportunity to escape, and that you have him at the appointed place at the appointed time.)

That you so be kept, Jesús María Martínez, until . . . (Mr. Clerk, on what day of the month does Friday about four weeks from this time come? May thirteenth, your honor.)

Very well, until Friday, the thirteenth of May, when you will be taken by the sheriff from your place of confinement to some safe and convenient spot within the county— that is in your discretion, Mr. Sheriff, you are only confined to the limits of the county—and that you there be hanged by the neck until you are dead; and the court was about to add, Jesús María Martínez, "May God have mercy on your soul," but the court will not assume the responsibility of asking an all-wise Providence to do that which a jury of your peers has refused to do. The Lord will not have mercy on your soul.

However, if you affect any religious belief, or are connected with any religious organization, it might be well for you to send for your priest or your minister and get from him such consolation as you can, but the court advises you to place no reliance upon anything of that kind.

Mr. Sheriff—remove the prisoner.

In spite of the popular belief that the condemned man escaped, he was hanged on schedule.

Threat from the South

During the first decade of its existence, Fort Union consisted of a shabby collection of log buildings at the west edge of a broad valley from which U.S. dragoons and mounted riflemen conducted far-reaching campaigns against Apaches, Utes, Kiowas, Comanches, and other nomadic Indian tribes and provided escort service for stagecoaches and mail wagons on the Santa Fe Trail. Like most military posts in the Southwest, the buildings were not enclosed by a wall.

Some of the officers and men were from southern states, and with the outbreak of the Civil War in the spring of 1861, many of them resigned from Federal service and headed home to offer their services to the Confederacy. New Mexico seemed far removed from the scenes of conflict, but the Territory was shaken in July 1861 when a Confederate force of more than 300 mounted riflemen from Texas, under the command of Lt. Col. John R. Baylor, moved north from Fort Bliss, Texas, occupied the southern New Mexico town of Mesilla, and captured the 700 Federal soldiers at nearby Fort Fillmore without firing a shot. On August 1, Lt. Col. Baylor proclaimed the establishment of the Confederate States' Territory of Arizona, embracing all of southern New Mexico, with its capital at Mesilla.

Government officials in Santa Fe, fearing a Confederate thrust to the north, called civilian men to the colors; the First Regiment of New Mexico Volunteers was organized and placed under the command of Col. Kit Carson. Commissioned a captain of volunteers in Las Vegas was Arthur Morrison, a multilingual German Jew (his surname originally was Marko) who had converted to Catholicism upon his marriage to a Hispanic woman in Las Vegas. Capt. Morrison raised a company of Las Vegas volunteers, consisting mostly of young Hispanic men.

The Las Vegas volunteers were sent twenty-five miles north to Fort Union to assist other New Mexico Volunteers and regular troops in building a massive earthen fortification a short distance east of the existing and undefensible complex of log buildings that had never been in danger of enemy attack. The new Fort Union, completed in August, was called the Star Fort, as the earthen embankments resembled a five-pointed star. From here, many of the volunteers were sent some two hundred miles to the southwest to reinforce Fort Craig on the Rio Grande, about midway between Santa Fe and Confederate-occupied Mesilla.

The Confederate thrust into northern New Mexico began in February 1862, when the Texas Brigade, some 3,000 volunteers under the command of Gen. Hopkins H. Sibley, began moving north from Mesilla. Only heavily garrisoned Fort Craig blocked the way to Santa Fe.

On February 21, Federal troops and New Mexico Volunteers at Fort Craig intercepted the Confederate force at Valverde, a Rio Grande fording place just north of the fort, but

A portion of Fort Union when the military post was regarded as "the guardian of the Santa Fe Trail." (Courtesy Museum of New Mexico, negative 1835)

retreated to the fort after a bloody all-day battle on the river's edge. The large Confederate force continued north to occupy Socorro and Albuquerque, and began the occupation of Santa Fe, the capital city, on March 10.

As the Confederate troops were approaching Santa Fe, Gov. Henry Connelly, a former Las Vegas resident, packed his belongings and moved the executive offices up the Santa Fe Trail to Las Vegas. On March 4 he established a temporary New Mexico capital in the Exchange Hotel on the Las Vegas plaza, a building he had helped to erect a decade before.

Gov. Connelly asked Gov. William Gilpin of the Territory of Colorado for help in halting the Confederate invasion, as it was apparent that the Texas Brigade planned to move up the Santa Fe Trail through Las Vegas, capture the lightly defended Fort Union, and continue north to take over the rich gold-mining fields in Colorado. Las Vegas, having survived the impacts of foreign armies, foreign traders, and Indian raiders down the Santa Fe Trail from the north, now braced itself for the impact of a foreign army coming up the trail from the south. But help was on the way from Colorado.

The First Regiment of Colorado Volunteers, under the command of Col. John P. Slough, a lawyer, arrived at Fort Union on March 10, and Col. Slough assumed command of all troops at the fort, including the garrison of about 400 regulars and the same number of New Mexico Volunteers. Here the Colorado troops, called "Pike's Peakers," were supplied and equipped with regulation clothing, arms, and ammunition from government stores.

With the intention of surprising the Confederates in Santa Fe and driving them from the city, Col. Slough left Fort Union on March 22 with 1,342 men, including Colorado and New

Mexico volunteers, units of regular infantry and cavalry, and two light artillery batteries. They camped on the night of March 23 in a large corral at Las Vegas and continued on down the Santa Fe Trail the next day. Anxiously, Las Vegas awaited news of the impending clash of Union and Confederate forces. It was not long in coming.

In a series of two Santa Fe Trail engagements in and near Glorieta Pass less than twenty miles out of Santa Fe, it was learned, the Confederate advance up the trail had been halted and the Texans were in full retreat. On March 26, advance units of the opposing forces had clashed where the trail passed through the narrow confines of Apache Canyon, and on March 28 the battle was resumed a few miles east at Pigeon's Ranch, a trail hostelry owned by Alexander Valle.

While the battle at Pigeon's Ranch was in progress, Maj. John P. Chivington, the "Fighting Parson" of the Colorado Volunteers, had circled around the Confederate lines with a force of more than 400 men. They attacked and burned the lightly guarded Confederate supply train of sixty to eighty wagons that was parked at Cañoncito, and bayoneted to death all the horses and mules used as draft animals. With the loss of all their provisions, the Texans began a long and weary retreat home. The Confederate Army had been within forty-five miles of Las Vegas when it was turned back.

By the end of April, Gov. Connelly had closed his executive offices in the Las Vegas hotel and had re-established them in the capital city, ending the brief tenure of Las Vegas as the capital of New Mexico. The Civil War was over as far as New Mexico was concerned, but it was followed by a new surge of military activity in the Territory as volunteer troops turned their attention to subduing hostile Indian tribes that had taken advantage of the Civil War chaos to step up their raiding forays. Meanwhile, nearly 2,000 California Volunteers, after a long march across the southern Arizona deserts, arrived in New Mexico in July 1862, intending to do battle with Confederate forces but arriving too late. The Confederates already had retreated into Texas.

Gen. James H. Carleton, commander of the California Column, became commander of all military forces in New Mexico late that year. From his headquarters in Santa Fe, he formulated plans to strengthen existing military forts and build new ones in preparation for military campaigns against the Mescalero Apaches, Navajos, Kiowas, and Comanches.

Construction of a new (the third) and greatly expanded Fort Union was started in 1863 adjacent to the earthen Star Fort, a building project that brought employment and additional market outlets for Las Vegas laborers, farmers, ranchers, and mill operators. By the time it was completed six years later, Fort Union consisted of a vast array of adobe brick buildings on stone foundations with towering brick chimneys, attractively situated around a huge parade ground in the center of the valley.

Las Vegas also became a supply center for two smaller forts that were erected in 1863 south and east of the community. Fort Bascom, a Fort Union satellite, was erected on the Canadian River about eighty-five miles to the east as a base for campaigns against the Kiowas and Comanches. Fort Sumner was erected on the newly-established Bosque Redondo Indian Reservation on the Pecos River about 100 miles south of Las Vegas, where Gen. Carleton planned to relocate the Mescalero Apache and Navajo tribes.

The task of rounding up the tribes in their traditional

homelands for removal to the new reservation was given to troops under the command of Col. Carson, who reportedly was not too happy about the assignment. Nevertheless, by 1865 there were more than 8,000 Navajos and 500 Mescalero Apaches held captive at the Bosque Redondo under the watchful eyes of soldiers at Fort Sumner.

The Navajo-Apache relocation project was a dismal failure. The Apaches fled the reservation and returned to their homes in south central New Mexico, and Gen. William Tecumseh Sherman, visiting Fort Sumner in 1868, arranged for the Navajos to be returned to their homelands far to the west. By 1870, both Fort Bascom and Fort Sumner were abandoned, but Fort Union remained a near and important neighbor to Las Vegas until its abandonment in 1891.

The Hermit

Of all those who journeyed down the Santa Fe Trail to New Mexico, none excited more attention in Las Vegas than an Italian recluse who became known among the Hispanic villagers as El Ermitano, The Hermit. His name was Giovanni Maria Agostini, or something close to that, and he arrived in Las Vegas one day in 1863 walking alongside a wagon train owned by Manuel Romero of Las Vegas. Slender, gaunt, and in his early sixties, he wore a long, black cape over his shoulders and steadied his steps with a long staff to which was fastened a small, tinkling bell.

He had approached Romero weeks before at a wagon camp at Council Grove, Kansas, and had asked permission to accompany him to New Mexico. Offered a ride on one of the wagons, he said he preferred to walk the hundreds of miles alongside the train. During the trek across the plains to New Mexico, Romero learned something of the stranger's background.

Born in northern Italy in 1801 of noble parentage, Agostini had received a good education in his native land and studied for the priesthood, but did not complete his studies

Giovanni Maria Agostini, "The Hermit," who walked the Santa Fe Trail to Las Vegas to find solitude on a mountain peak. (Courtesy Museum of New Mexico, negative 110764)

because he disagreed with some aspects of Roman Catholic doctrine. By the time he was thirty, he had embarked upon his life as a solitary wanderer on three continents.

After five years of walking around Spain, visiting the various religious shrines and sanctuaries, he traveled across the Atlantic to South America and spent the next twenty years wandering the length and breadth of that continent, visiting various Indian tribes and pausing at intervals to live in remote caves. From there he journeyed north to Central America and Mexico, Cuba, Canada, and the United States, turning up in 1863 at the wagon rendezvous point at Council Grove.

Upon their arrival at Las Vegas, Romero offered his new friend the comforts of his large home. Agostini accepted this, but made it clear that he preferred the hard ground to a comfortable bed and that the only nourishment he wanted or needed was cornmeal mush.

Word soon spread around town that Romero was playing host to a holy man, healer, and miracle worker. Agostini, it is said, never claimed to be any of these things, but the villagers believed his unusual appearance and demeanor proclaimed him as such. To escape the crowds that gathered around him in Las Vegas, Agostini walked down the Santa Fe Trail a few miles to the site of the future village of Romeroville, and finding a cave in the wall of a small canyon, moved in. Even there he could not find the solitude he wanted, as villagers from miles around, referring to him as Juan Bautista, or John the Baptist, converged on the cave to ask and receive his advice and council, some of them camping for days in front of the cave.

Eyeing the 10,263-foot summit of Cerro del Tecolote, Owl Peak, in the Sangre de Cristo Mountains eighteen miles northwest of Las Vegas, Agostini decided that a lofty home high above the surrounding countryside would provide him the peace and solitude he desired. After a difficult climb up the timbered slopes of the mountain, known ever since as Hermit's Peak, he found a suitable abode in a small cave facing a ledge a few hundred feet below the summit.

Even there he was not always alone, for friends climbed the towering peak from time to time to visit him, often bringing cornmeal and asking his blessings. One group of men fashioned a windbreak in front of the Hermit's cave, to protect him from strong and chilling winds and wild animals. Later, they felled some trees and built him a small, windowless cabin over a spring on the flat summit.

Occasionally, the Hermit would descend the mountain from his primitive cabin to visit friends, including Romero, Teodoro Pena, and Arthur Morrison in Las Vegas and Samuel B. Watrous, who lived eighteen miles up the trail at La Junta, a village later to be renamed Watrous in honor of the original 1849 settler. The Hermit had an agreement with Watrous that he would build a fire at given intervals on the summit of the mountain, a fire Watrous could see from his home, as a signal that he was alive and well. Only if a fire failed to appear after a given interval was there to be cause for alarm.

Early in 1867, after living atop the mountain for nearly four years, the Hermit descended to Las Vegas and announced that he was moving on—that he planned to walk south to Mexico. Bidding adieu to his many friends, he disappeared on foot down the Santa Fe Trail.

It is doubtful that the Hermit crossed the border into Mexico as he had planned. He was seen periodically in the southern New Mexico community of Mesilla and in El Paso,

Hermit's Peak, near Las Vegas, with the Gallinas River in the foreground.
(Courtesy Museum of New Mexico, Jesse Nusbaum photo, negative 61278)

Texas, to the south, and for a while apparently found a remote abode in the Hueco Mountains east of El Paso. During this period he was befriended by Col. Albert J. Fountain of Mesilla and El Paso, a prominent lawyer and world traveler who had arrived in New Mexico in 1862 with the California Volunteers.

While visiting Mesilla in April 1869, the Hermit announced that he intended to climb into the jagged-topped Organ Mountains east of the town, and that upon reaching the highest peak he would light a signal fire at night to inform friends that he had reached that point safely. Col. Fountain and others warned him that he was entering Apache domain, but the Hermit could not be dissuaded from his purpose.

Time went by, no signal fire appeared, and a search party was organized in Mesilla to enter the mountains in an effort to find the wanderer. The closing chapter was told in a brief newspaper article published in *The New Mexican* at Santa Fe on May 10, 1869, which said:

> *The remains of the Italian recluse, who, for the past six years, has lived in the mountains of New Mexico, was brought brought to Mesilla on the second inst. (May 2). He was killed by Indians in the Organ Mountains, and had apparently been dead six or eight days. His mode of life proclaimed him as a zealot. He was known by the Mexicans as the Hermitano.*

Trail Recollections

Commercial and military traffic on the Santa Fe Trail increased in intensity during the Civil War era, with an estimated 3,000 wagons passing through Las Vegas in 1865 and some 5,000 in 1866. Sounds of cracking whips and shouted commands echoed through the dusty streets of the adobe village as wagon drivers urged their ox and mule teams forward at a sluggish pace of ten to fifteen miles a day. By now, most of the southbound Conestoga prairie schooners were bypassing Santa Fe and proceeding south down the Chihuahua Trail through El Paso to richer markets in the interior of the Republic of Mexico.

Concord stagecoaches, carrying travelers and emigrants who could afford the $200 fare between the Missouri frontier and Santa Fe, paused briefly in the town before rolling on to their destinations. Unlike the Oregon Trail and other wagon trails that pierced the Western frontier, the Santa Fe Trail was principally a commercial and military thoroughfare, and saw but few emigrant trains.

In Las Vegas, the Romeros and the Bacas were among the Hispanic families who entered the lucrative Santa Fe trade, put wagon trains on the trail, and established profitable mercantile businesses. Some Las Vegas pioneers left recollections and journals to their families and descendants describing their experiences on the trail.

Ricardo Gonzales, who lived on a sheep ranch northeast of Las Vegas, told his family how Hispanic sheep ranchers from over a wide area of northeastern New Mexico banded together in the spring of 1868 to haul their wool up the Trail to Eastern markets in a train of 200 ox-drawn wagons. The ranchers had no sacks, and the wool was thrown into the wagons in loose bulk, tramped down, and covered with sheets.

The wagon train began moving up the trail on May 1, Gonzales said, arranged in two parallel columns of 100 wagons each, with horses and extra oxen walking between the two columns. He estimated that the wool caravan included at least 3,200 oxen, more than 500 horses and mules, and about 500 men. About 100 of the men rode horseback in front of the caravan, guiding the train and watching for hostile Indians. Transporting the most wool in the caravan were Rumaldo Baca of Las Vegas, who had thirty wagons and at least 500 oxen; and José Manuel Gonzales, who had twelve wagons, each drawn by from eight to twelve yokes of oxen.

The Arkansas River in Kansas was flooded when the wagon train reached it according to Gonzales, and the caravan rested on the south bank for three days before attempting a crossing. The difficult crossing took six days, and fourteen pairs of oxen were hitched to each wagon in order to pull the heavy loads across the swollen river. As the wool caravan reached each of the newly established military forts along the trail in Kansas, escorts of up to eighty U.S. soldiers would accompany the train to the next fort. The wool shipping venture was a financial success, Gonzales said; the empty wagons returned to New Mexico in October.

Charles A. Blanchard, a French Canadian from Montreal who settled in Las Vegas in the mid-1860s, left his family a lengthy manuscript detailing some of his experiences on the Santa Fe Trail. He included a remarkable story of heroism during an outbreak of Indian hostilities in Kansas.

In the summer of 1868, Blanchard wrote, he was a member of a small wagon train that hauled loose wool up the trail to the new town of Ellsworth, Kansas, end-of-track of the westward pushing Kansas Pacific Railroad. Reaching Ellsworth in July, he sold his wool and traded his ox team and $2,000 in cash for sixty-six mules and ten wagons. He and the twelve New Mexicans with him then headed back down the trail toward Las Vegas. On August 19, while camped on the site of present Garden City, Kansas, nearly 100 mounted Indians swooped down on them and ran off all their mules and horses. None of the party was killed, but all were left stranded on the prairie.

Blanchard wrote that he left the camp late that afternoon and walked to Fort Dodge, about fifty miles to the east, arriving there early the next morning. He said that Capt. Douglas, the commanding officer, furnished him an escort of soldiers and some animals to retrieve the stranded train and return it to the fort.

Blanchard and his companions were ordered to establish camp two miles east of Fort Dodge and to remain there until it was considered safe to resume their journey to New Mexico. They remained in this camp until October 13, during which time the Indian war raged all around them and brought traffic on the Trail to a standstill.

Blanchard wrote that the Indians in Kansas, restless because the government had failed to deliver promised food and supplies under treaty provisions, went on the warpath in August when a desperado known as Dutch Henry shot down two Indian women in cold blood near Fort Dodge. Cheyenne, Arapaho, Comanche, Kiowa, and Ute Indians began attacking and destroying wagon trains on the trail with increasing fury.

While camped outside Fort Dodge, and near the end of their stay, Blanchard and his companions were visited one evening by a veteran Indian scout known as Uncle Ned White. Blanchard wrote that Uncle Ned sat down at the campfire, filled his pipe, and proceeded to tell them of a remarkable incident he had just witnessed. According to Uncle Ned's story, as passed along by Blanchard, a small wagon train, moving west along the Santa Fe Trail, halted late one afternoon in September 1868 on the north bank of the Arkansas River some miles east of Fort Dodge. Bill Simpson, the wagon boss, ordered his men to make camp because the train could not possibly reach the fort that day.

There was one passenger on the wagon train, a Mrs. Updyke, who was en route to Fort Dodge to join her officer husband. She was impatient and wanted to ride on alone to the fort, but Simpson would not permit it, warning her that she might never get there alive. Soon after they had camped, a swarthy horseman whom Simpson recognized as Black Jack, a notorious cut-throat who sometimes led bands of Indians in attacks on wagon trains, approached the camp and asked for some "tabacker" and whisky. Being refused, he departed after eyeing Mrs. Updyke.

"This means Indians," Simpson said. "Who will ride to the fort for help?"

The first to volunteer was Kirk Gordon, a young plains-man and hunter who was serving as Simpson's chief assistant and guide. As Gordon sped off to the fort for assistance, Simpson gave orders to circle the wagons in preparation for an Indian attack.

Within a short time, an estimated 2,000 mounted Indians attacked the fortified wagon train and the outnumbered wag-oners fought for their lives. At the height of the battle, three companies of cavalry appeared on the western horizon, and the Indians began to withdraw. When the attack started, Mrs. Updyke had been hidden in a wagon under some blankets and robes. When the Indians withdrew, it was discovered that she was missing, and moments later she was seen being carried off by an Indian on horseback.

The cavalrymen from the fort, who had halted on a ridge with the Indians between them and the circled wagons, were under the command of Lt. Updyke, the captured woman's husband. He watched helplessly and silently as the Indians rode off with his wife, and sent a courier back to the fort for reinforcements.

The Indians formed a huge half-circle just out of rifle shot from the soldiers, the open end facing the cavalrymen. Two of the Indians took Mrs. Updyke into the center of the half-circle and began torturing her with arrows, hoping to draw the soldiers into a trap. As the woman's screams echoed across the prairie, Kirk Gordon turned to Lt. Updyke and asked him why he didn't order a charge. The cavalry officer, great beads of cold perspiration oozing from his forehead, hesitated before answering.

"No, it would be a foolish sacrifice of my men," he said. "They would all be killed."

Gordon, six feet tall, dressed in a blue shirt and old yellow overalls, with a pistol hanging from each hip, turned his horse around and started riding slowly down the ridge toward the Indians. "Both soldiers and Indians gazed at his determined approach, spellbound by that unique combination of curiosity and admiration which sometimes enthralls great bodies of men with its hypnotic power," Blanchard wrote. "Not a sound was heard, even the breeze died away. The setting sun brought out in queer relief the slowly advancing horseman. The lengthening shadow of horse and rider seemed to grow in size like an avenging demon."

Gordon rode slowly into the "jaws of death" until he had reached a point about 100 yards from the awed and silent figures of Mrs. Updyke and her two captors. Then, spurring his horse into a burst of speed, he shot the two captors, swept the woman onto his horse, wheeled his horse around quickly, and sped back toward the cavalry position. As he swept the woman off her feet he slid to the rear of his horse, placed her in the saddle, then turned around facing the Indians, a gun in each hand, his back against Mrs. Updyke's back. "Stick to the horse whatever happens," Gordon shouted to the woman.

As they sped away, back to back, Gordon emptied his guns at the Indians who had suddenly come to life and were in close pursuit. Mrs. Updyke could hear the sickening plunk of Indian bullets as they buried themselves in the body of her protector.

Cavalry reinforcements from the fort arrived on the scene as the drama was concluding and charged down the hill to scatter the Indians. As Gordon's fleet horse and its two riders reached the cavalry position, Gordon slumped over and fell dead to the ground. Lt. Updyke rushed forward to embrace his wife, but she dropped to her knees and cradled the head of her lifeless rescuer in her lap, her tears bathing his face.

Gen. Phil Sheridan, commander of the reinforcements, watched the touching scene silently. A trooper picked up Gordon's Scottish cap off the ground and handed it to the general. Gen. Sheridan dismounted, removed his hat, took Gordon's cap and walked to the body of the dead hero. Tenderly, he placed the cap over the dead man's brow and looked into the lifeless face.

"Kirk Gordon," the general said softly, "you are the bravest man who ever lived."

Blanchard and his companions left Fort Dodge on October 13 with a wagon train headed for Las Vegas after signing releases waiving any claims against the government for losses suffered in Indian attacks on the way home. He wrote that the government awarded him $9,000 for his previous losses, giving him half the amount at intervals over a five-year period and the other half in 1908—forty years later.

At about the time Blanchard and his companions were arriving home in Las Vegas, a small ceremony was occurring in eastern Kansas that was to mark the beginning of the end of the Santa Fe Trail. It was a blustery morning in Topeka on October 30, 1868, when a small and rather skeptical group of spectators gathered near the south bank of the Kansas River to watch groundbreaking ceremonies for a new railroad. Sen. Edmund G. Ross of Kansas, later to become a New Mexico governor, gave a short speech predicting great things for the railroad.

Col. Cyrus K. Holliday, founder of the new railroad, climbed up on the seat of a livery hack and declared that his line someday would extend from Chicago all the way to the

Pacific Ocean, by way of Santa Fe. The onlookers remained skeptical.

Sen. Ross then picked up a spade and scooped some dirt from the ground, and construction of the Atchison, Topeka and Santa Fe Railroad was under way. But it would be more than ten years before the steel rails, inching down the wagon road, reached Las Vegas.

The Shrinking Trail

The expansion of Fort Union during the 1860s into a major military post and supply center for other forts brought a measure of security to the lower reaches of the Santa Fe Trail. Soldiers from the fort and its satellite military posts conducted relentless and far-reaching campaigns against hostile bands of Apaches, Utes, Kiowas, and Comanches, driving the Indians from the region and making the New Mexico portion of the Trail safe for travelers.

The Fort Union expansion, with its increasing demand for locally supplied agricultural produce and building materials, also brought a surge of prosperity and new settlers to the region. In 1864, the seat of San Miguel County was moved from decaying San Miguel del Bado up the Trail to growing Las Vegas, most of the county records disappearing along the way.

As the Indian danger abated, new settlements began springing up on the plains south of Las Vegas and in the mountains to the north and west. Hispanic sheep ranchers drove their flocks east from the Rio Grande Valley and established the village of Puerto de Luna, named for the Luna family, on the banks of the Pecos River about seventy-five miles south of Las Vegas. The abandoned buildings of Fort Sumner, another forty miles down the stream, were purchased by Lucien B. Maxwell, former owner of the huge Maxwell Land Grant in northern New Mexico, who transformed the former military post into a farm and ranch village called Fort Sumner. He established his residence in the building that had served as officers' quarters.

South of Fort Sumner, by the early 1870s, John S. Chisum was running 80,000 head of cattle along a one-hundred-mile stretch of the Pecos River, the first Texan to move Longhorn cattle into the broad and uninhabited valley. A wagon road was established from Las Vegas south through the new settlements to the Chisum ranch headquarters.

Mineral discoveries in the mountains north and west of Las Vegas brought a flurry of prospectors and mine speculators to the region. Mining camps sprang up almost overnight in scattered and isolated locations with each gold or silver strike.

Cattlemen, sheepmen, soldiers, miners, prospectors—they all needed supplies, and Las Vegas, astride the Santa Fe Trail with its incoming wagon caravans of trade goods, was where most went to get them.

Las Vegas took on a cosmopolitan atmosphere as increasing numbers of foreign-born immigrants settled in the town alongside the Hispanic pioneers. Some of the first to envision economic opportunity in Las Vegas were numbers of German Jewish immigrants who penetrated the Western frontier following their arrival in the United States. Among the most successful of these were Emanuel Rosenwald and Charles Ilfeld.

South side of the Las Vegas Plaza in the 1870s. (Courtesy Museum of New Mexico, James N. Furlong photo, negative 42326)

Rosenwald, who arrived in the United States from Bavaria in 1853, arrived in Las Vegas in 1862 from Colorado, where he had been trading among the Indians. In Las Vegas he established a successful mercantile business that eventually became known as E. Rosenwald and Son.

Ilfeld was employed by Adolph Letcher at a store in Taos in 1867 when the two decided that Las Vegas offered greater opportunities. In the spring of that year they loaded their merchandise on the backs of 100 burros and guided the awkward caravan over the mountains and south through the Mora Valley to Las Vegas, where they opened a store on the plaza. Ilfeld, who slept under the counter of the store to protect it from thieves, bought Letcher's interest in 1874, and the Charles Ilfeld Co. eventually became the largest mercantile firm in New Mexico.

Also adding to the cosmopolitan atmosphere of the former Mexican village were immigrants from other European countries. Alexander Grzelachowski, a Roman Catholic priest from Poland who had served various parishes in New Mexico, left the priesthood to engage in the mercantile business on the Las Vegas plaza. A.V. Aoy, a native of Spain who came to the United States by way of Cuba and Mexico, decided that Las Vegas needed a newspaper, and in spite of his limited knowledge of English and the printing trade, launched the town's first newspaper, *The Acorn,* in December 1869. It was a weekly published in both English and Spanish.

A second newspaper, the *Las Vegas Mail,* was established in 1871 by S.H. Newman and W.N. Bollinger. Editor Newman soon was convicted of publishing libelous statements about U.S. Attorney Thomas B. Catron of Santa Fe. Unable to pay the fine, he tried in vain to edit the paper from his Las Vegas jail cell.

German-born Louis Hommel of Las Vegas, who had served as a bugler with the New Mexico Volunteers during the Civil War, bought the *Mail* plant and launched the *Las Vegas Gazette,* but he, too, had his problems. He was charged with assault, released on bail, and while free on bond he was charged with stealing a horse. Struggling with a deputy sheriff who came to arrest him, Hommel shot and killed the deputy and was convicted of a murder charge. He was pardoned by New Mexico Gov. Lew Wallace.

J.H. Koogler, from Iowa, took over the *Gazette* in about 1875. Under his direction, for nearly a decade, it was considered one of the leading newspapers of New Mexico.

W. Scott Moore, a retired railroad freight conductor, bought the hot springs six miles north of Las Vegas in the 1870s. The springs were known locally as the Montezuma Hot Springs because of a legend that Montezuma had bathed in the springs on his way to Mexico to found the Aztec Empire. Moore built a small health spa hotel known as The Adobe House. Moore was just one of a long succession of owners and operators of the popular hot springs.

By the late 1870s, Las Vegas was a thriving trade center of more than 2,000 inhabitants, with substantial mercantile houses and a few hotels, saloons and gambling halls. Meanwhile, the Santa Fe Trail had been shrinking from the east as Atchison, Topeka and Santa Fe construction crews put down mile after mile of steel rails westward across the Kansas prairies, each mile of track shortening the wagon road by the same distance.

As the Santa Fe and other railroads pushed west across Kansas in the 1870s, Texas cattle ranchers drove great herds of Longhorn cattle north to the Kansas railheads for shipment by rail to Eastern markets, creating a series of wild and rowdy

South Pacific Avenue, Las Vegas, in about 1879. (Courtesy Museum of New Mexico, James N. Furlong photo, negative 100863)

cattle towns along the rail lines that produced fearless lawmen, notorious outlaws, and some who were a little of both. Among the most violent of the cattle towns that sprang up along the railroad lines was Dodge City, Kansas, a few miles east of Fort Dodge, which was reached by the Santa Fe line in September 1872.

From there, Santa Fe officials had to choose which of the two main branches of the Santa Fe Trail to follow into New Mexico. The shorter route was the Cimarron Cut-Off, extending south and west across an uninhabited desert and entering New Mexico from the east near the present town of Clayton. The longer Mountain Branch continued west from Dodge City along the Arkansas River into Colorado and then veered southwest to cross into New Mexico over rugged Raton Pass on the Colorado-New Mexico border. The railroad chose the Mountain Branch, as it afforded needed coal deposits and water, and the region was deemed more suitable for new settlements than the Cimarron Desert on the shorter route.

The railroad crossed into southeastern Colorado in 1873, pushed on down through Las Animas and Trinidad, and reached the New Mexico line, near the summit of Raton Pass, on November 1, 1878. All that was left of the Santa Fe Trail was that portion of the wagon road remaining in New Mexico.

From the Colorado line, it was another 100 miles or so to Las Vegas, soon to become the first New Mexico town to feel the impact of the "iron horse." It was to be another eight months, however, before the tracks reached the town.

The Hanging Windmill

anuel Barela walked into the Flores Saloon in Las Vegas at sundown on June 4, 1879, one month before the railroad arrived in town, and asked for a pint of wine. He was in charge of a wagon train owned by his brother, Mariano Barela, a prominent merchant of Las Cruces in southern New Mexico, which had been camped just outside Las Vegas for several days. During that time, Barela had been whooping it up in Las Vegas, visiting the various saloons and gambling dens, and, as the *Las Vegas Gazette* reported, becoming very "demonstrative and disagreeable."

As the bartender was drawing Barela's pint of wine, the Las Cruces resident turned and noticed two men standing and talking just outside the saloon door. According to one report, Barela bet the bartender that he could shoot the third button off the vest of one of the men. At any rate, Barela drew his six-shooter and fired out the door. The bullet struck one of the men, Jesús Morales, in the face, inflicting a severe but not fatal wound.

Benigno Romero, seventy-year-old companion of the wounded man, was shocked by the unprovoked shooting of

Morales, and when Barela came to the door, Romero asked him why he had shot his friend. Barela answered by firing two shots into Romero's body, killing him instantly. Moments later, Las Vegas officers arrived on the scene, arrested Barela, and took him to jail. Many bystanders had witnessed the double shooting, and a large crowd of citizens followed the policemen and their prisoner to the jail, making angry threats to lynch the prisoner. The officers got Barela safely to jail and locked him in a cell. The angry citizens stood outside the closed doors of the jail for a while, hurling insults and threats at the prisoner, but the crowd soon melted away.

Referring to Romero, the man who had been slain, the *Las Vegas Gazette* said:

> *The person killed was a hardworking old man. He had stopped before the saloon to talk of his work next day. He was an entire stranger to Barela, and neither he nor his companion had given him the slightest pretext for offense. The shooting was entirely without provocation, a devilish and crazy freak which should not go unpunished.*

All available officers were placed on guard duty at the jail that night to safeguard the prisoner from any lynch mob. The evening passed quietly, however, with no sign of trouble. Then, at midnight, the silence was broken by the sounds of gun shots on a nearby hill. Somebody called for the police, and the policemen on guard duty at the jail rushed to the scene of the supposed trouble.

As soon as the officers had left, a large crowd of citizens moved silently upon the jail and overpowered the few guards left on duty. Two of them knocked at the door of the jail and informed the jailer that they had come to deliver a prisoner. When he opened the door, the mob moved in and overpowered him.

The citizens forced the jailer to hand over the keys to Barela's cell. They took Barela from his cell, and, apparently on second thought, also took custody of another prisoner, Giovanni Dugi, an Italian held on a murder charge. The two men were dragged to the barren plaza in the center of town.

Standing near the center of the plaza was an odd-shaped windmill, erected in 1876 over a well. Built entirely of wood, the windmill consisted of two parts, a large platform held about twenty feet above the ground by four sturdy posts and a narrowing superstructure that rose about another twenty feet from the platform. Wood ladders led up to the platform and on to the top.

In bright moonlight, Barela was hanged from the windmill, and when he expired, Dugi met the same fate. "In half a minute after the hanging was accomplished," the *Gazette* reported, "the plaza was perfectly clear of people and the town was as quiet as a graveyard."

It was at about this same time, according to Miguel A. Otero in his book, *My Life on the Frontier,* that the "hanging windmill" claimed yet another victim. Otero, a Las Vegas pioneer who served as governor of New Mexico from 1897 to 1906, identified this victim as a cowboy visitor named Beckworth who enjoyed demonstrating his skills at handling a pistol.

While twirling his pistol in his hand before an admiring audience, the gun went off and killed a man standing behind him. Beckworth apologized, saying that it was just an accident. He resumed his pistol twirling and the gun went off again, this

The "Hanging Windmill" on the Las Vegas Plaza served vigilantes as a handy scaffold until its demolition in 1880. (Courtesy Museum of New Mexico, James N. Furlong photo, negative 14386)

time killing a woman standing in the doorway of her house across the street. Again, Beckworth apologized, saying it was just an accident.

Officers quickly arrived on the scene and hauled Beckworth off to jail. He was found hanging from the windmill the next morning, Otero said, with a placard hanging from his neck which read: "This is no accident."

RAIL TOWN TALES

"Baca's Folly" turned out to be a poor commercial investment for its builder, Rumaldo Baca, when the railroad by-passed his Las Vegas property. (Courtesy Museum of New Mexico, negative 2478)

A New Town

Rumaldo Baca was among those Las Vegas residents who assumed that the approaching railroad line would enter the community and that a depot would be established on or near the plaza. As an investment, Baca erected an elaborate, four-story building near the center of town about where he thought the depot would be, with rooms he could rent for stores, offices, and meeting halls. The unpredictable Atchison, Topeka and Santa Fe Railroad Co., however, bypassed Las Vegas one mile to the east, selecting a spot in a wheatfield on the opposite bank of the Gallinas River as the site for its depot and yards. Baca's elaborate but unoccupied building became known locally as "Baca's Folly."

A townsite was staked out in the wheatfield, lots were sold, and by the time the steel rails arrived on the scene on July 1, 1879, a new town was taking shape in the form of hastily erected frame buildings and tents that housed stores, restaurants, saloons, and living quarters. The bustling new town was called East Las Vegas, while the original settlement on the opposite bank of the stream became known as West Las Vegas. In local parlance, the neighboring communities were often referred to as New Town and Old Town, the Eastside and the Westside. As soon as the tracks reached East Las Vegas, the railroad dismantled its temporary terminal buildings at the construction camp of Otero, about 100 miles up the line, loaded the material on flat cars, and shipped them to Las Vegas for reassembly. Russell A. Kistler, an itinerant journalist who had established a weekly newspaper called the *Otero Optic* at the construction camp in May, loaded his small plant on a freight car at the same time and hurried south to resume publication of his newspaper in East Las Vegas as the *Las Vegas Optic.*

Veteran track followers, those who anticipated golden opportunities at each new end-of-track town on the frontier, rode the rails to the new town and began setting up shop. In addition to legitimate business and professional men, the railroad brought a large assortment of frontier riffraff, including robbers, thieves, gamblers, swindlers (called bunko men), gunmen, and vagrants, many of them hell raisers from Dodge City and other Kansas cattle towns. Among these was Hyman G. Neill, alias Hoodoo Brown, who as the first justice of the peace in East Las Vegas became the virtual ruler of the new town with the help of his Kansas cronies.

The arrival of the railroad to Las Vegas, first end-of-track town in New Mexico, was celebrated in grand style on Independence Day 1879, by which time the tracks already were extending south beyond the new depot. The centers of social activities for the celebration were the old Exchange Hotel on the West Las Vegas plaza and the new Close and Patterson dance hall that had been erected in East Las Vegas on Railroad Avenue, a new street just to the west of and paralleling the railroad tracks. Grand balls were held at both establishments.

The Fourth of July dawned bright and clear. Farmers and ranchers from miles around streamed into the community during the morning hours on horseback, on foot, and in wagons, carriages, and buckboards. Business houses around the old plaza were decked out in flags and bunting. A speaker's platform, decorated with evergreen boughs, was erected in the plaza for the big occasion.

The crowds took in the sights on the plaza, then forded the shallow stream to inspect the two steam locomotives, decorated with flags and furbelows, which had been pulled up in front of the depot. For most, it was their first sight of a steam locomotive. All awaited eagerly the arrival of the first train into East Las Vegas, a special excursion train that railroad officials had arranged to bring excursionists down the line from Trinidad, Colorado.

The oratory on the plaza was scheduled to begin at 2 o'clock, but was delayed for one hour by an early afternoon thundershower. The wind was still blowing when the speech-making got under way. The principal speaker was Gen. G.A. Smith of Santa Fe, collector of internal revenue for New Mexico, who hailed the coming of the railroad as the greatest of civilizers.

The New Mexican at Santa Fe, reporting on Gen. Smith's speech at Las Vegas, said that "he congratulated the people not only of Las Vegas, but of the territory, upon the completion of the railroad to this point, and hailed it as a great civilizer and additional evidence of our greatness as a nation." The type of "civilization" the railroad brought to Las Vegas soon became quite evident.

Jesse James and Doc Holliday

$\mathcal{S}$aturday night, July 26, 1879, saw the grand opening of a number of new saloons, gambling halls, and other places of amusement in East Las Vegas. Announcements of the openings were duly reported in the newspapers, on street posters, and by word of mouth, and the new railroad community bulged at the seams that night as the crowds poured in. The *Weekly New Mexican* at Santa Fe, on August 2, described the Las Vegas scene this way:

> *The crowd needs no description. The merchant from the east in broad cloth, jostled the laborer, while the soft handed clerk had for his neighbor a cowboy, whose wide brimmed hat with glittering cord, and cartridge belt set off his good looks to best advantage. Contractors, traders, ranchmen, speculators, etc, etc., were there in force. The women who did the dancing were American and Mexican ranging through nearly all grades of good and bad looks. The halls were brilliantly lighted, music was furnished by excellent string bands for the dancers, glasses jingled in time with the music and as was to have been expected many of*

the pleasure seekers were more than half seas over before the
night turned toward the wee small hours.

Jesse James, the notorious Missouri outlaw, may have
been among the celebrants that night, for it was later learned
that he was in town that day. His brief visit was mentioned
months later by the *Las Vegas Optic,* which published this brief
item on December 8, 1879: "Jesse James was a guest at the
Las Vegas Hot Springs from July 26th to 29th. Of course it was
not generally known."

One who claimed to have known at the time was Henry
F. Hoyt, itinerant physician and surveyor who was working in
1879 as a bartender at the Exchange Hotel in Las Vegas. In
his book, *A Frontier Doctor,* published in 1929, Hoyt told of
riding north from town to the hot springs resort for a Sunday
dinner and finding his friend Billy the Kid, whom he had met
previously on the cattle ranges, in the dining room with another man the Kid introduced to him as "Mr. Howard from
Tennessee." Hoyt said the Kid confided to him after dinner
that "Mr. Howard" actually was Jesse James, who was in
seclusion and had come to the hot springs to visit his old
friends, Mr. and Mrs. W. Scott Moore, owners and operators
of the resort.

Billy the Kid, who had come to Las Vegas to see the
railroad, also knew the Moores, who introduced him to their
other guest. Hoyt wrote that James made a tentative offer to
the Kid that they "join forces and hit the trail together," but
that the Kid turned down the proposal, as armed robbery was
not one of his trades.

Miguel A. Otero also claimed to have visited with Jesse
James at the hot springs resort that Sunday, but he didn't say

anything about seeing Dr. Hoyt or Billy the Kid there. In his book, *My Life on the Frontier,* Otero wrote that Moore introduced him to Jesse James on condition that he keep the visitor's identity a secret. He said that Moore had grown up with the James boys in Missouri.

Otero said that James was a quiet and unobtrusive visitor, in appearance and dress looking more like an ordinary businessman than a noted desperado. He said he believed it was James' first and only trip to New Mexico, and that he had come for a weekend rest with the notion that he might locate under an assumed name in New Mexico, Arizona, or the Republic of Mexico in an effort to live a peaceful and quiet life with his family. He said the outlaw left Las Vegas by train as quietly as he had come.

Meanwhile, sounds of gunfire interrupted the festivities during the July 26 grand openings in East Las Vegas as the new town recorded its first fatal shooting. The victim was Mike Gordon, a former U.S. Fifth Cavalry scout, who went looking for trouble and found it.

Gordon had started his celebrating a little early, for the *Las Vegas Gazette* said that he had been drinking heavily for several days. Once during the evening he threatened to shoot out all the lights in a big new dance hall on Railroad Avenue, but decided it was too big a job and left without trying.

Gordon walked over to another dance hall on Centre Street, where his girlfriend was working. The newspaper did not identify her by name, saying only that she was "the woman with whom he had lived a great part of the time for several years." He tried to persuade the woman to accompany him back to the dance on Railroad Avenue, where a larger crowd had congregated. She refused, and he walked out of the hall alone, muttering that he was determined to kill somebody or be killed himself before morning.

The killing of Mike Gordon occurred moments later just outside the Centre Street dance hall. The *Gazette* said that it was difficult to ascertain how the tragedy occurred, adding:

> *Gordon was standing in the street to the right of the hall after some of his threats and drew a revolver and fired, the bullet passing through the pants legs of a Mexican and struck in the floor in line with the bartender who was standing at the rear of the bar.*
>
> *Other shots were fired immediately but it is difficult to tell how or who by.*
>
> *It is said that Gordon fired a second shot. Every person there says three shots were fired, while several maintain that five in all were fired.*
>
> *Gordon at once ceased firing and disappeared. An hour or two later a Mr. Kennedy went into his tent, some thirty or forty yards away, to go to bed and hearing groans investigated and found Gordon laying on the ground out-side. The news soon spread and his woman arriving on the ground had him taken to her room east of the Court house, where he died at 6 o'clock Sunday morning. In the after-noon the Coroner held an inquest and the jury returned a verdict of excusable homicide.*

Gordon had been shot through the chest, the bullet emerging below his shoulder blade.

The *Gazette* identified Gordon as a Fifth Cavalry veteran who had scouted the plains and mountains for fourteen years, had visited most of the Western mining camps, and was considered a bad man only when drinking. The *Optic* said that Gordon was "known to have rescued white people from the savage Indians" before liquor got the better of him, adding:

> *Of late years, Gordon had been disfigured by the loss of his nose. It was bitten off by a gambler from whom he was taking money. His antagonist seized him with a grasp of iron by both ears and with his teeth wrought the disfiguration.*

The *Gazette* said a crowd witnessed all the shooting outside the dance hall, but nobody seemed to know who was doing it. Or at least, nobody would say who was doing it. Maybe it was because the killer was John H. "Doc" Holliday, consumptive dentist, gambler, and gunman who operated a saloon and gambling hall on Centre Street in partnership with Jordan L. Webb.

Two years later, on July 20, 1881, the *Optic* referred to an item in the *Arizona Democrat* saying that Doc Holliday had been accused of stagecoach robbery near Tombstone, Arizona. The *Optic* said the item should be of interest to old-timers of Las Vegas, adding:

> *It will be remembered, especially by the pioneers of the East Side, that Doc Holliday was at one time the keeper of a gin-mill on Centre Street, near the present site of the Centre Street bakery. Doc was always considered a shiftless, bagged-legged character—a killer and professional cut-throat and not a whit too refined to rob stages or even steal sheep. He is the identical individual who killed poor, inoffensive Mike Gordon and crept through one of the many*

legal loop-holes that characterized Hoodoo Brown's judicial dispensation.

Holliday, an 1872 graduate of the Pennsylvania College of Dental Surgery, headed west from his native Georgia in the early 1870s when doctors told him he had chronic pulmonary tuberculosis and advised him to seek a drier climate. He practiced dentistry in Dallas, Texas, and becoming adept at poker and monte; he gave up his practice there in 1875 to embark on a life as a frontier gambler and part-time dentist.

In succeeding years he became a familiar figure in Colorado and Black Hills mining towns and in Dodge City, Kansas, gambling, coughing, and achieving the reputation, deserved or not, of a deadly gunfighter. In Dodge City he opened a dental office and became a good friend of the controversial lawman, Wyatt Earp.

Holliday arrived in Las Vegas months ahead of the railroad, for San Miguel County court records show that he was fined $25 during the March term of court in 1879 for keeping an illegal gaming table. He opened his last dental office in Las Vegas in the spring of 1879, apparently abandoning his dental practice when he opened his saloon and gambling hall in East Las Vegas in July.

Wyatt Earp and his brother, James, joined Holliday in Las Vegas in the fall of 1879, and there is evidence that Wyatt purchased an interest in or worked at Holliday's gambling establishment. The *Optic* referred to Earp that fall as "one of the hoodoo fellers of Las Vegas," indicating an association with Hoodoo Brown. Holliday and the two Earp brothers apparently left Las Vegas at about the end of the year.

Holliday paid at least one more visit to Las Vegas, accord-

*John H. "Doc" Holliday, who killed "poor, inoffensive" Mike Gordon in
Las Vegas. (Courtesy University of Oklahoma Library, Western History Collections,
Rose No. 1817)*

ing to Miguel A. Otero in his book, *My Life on the Frontier*. In 1880, while passing through Las Vegas on a southbound train, Holliday got off the train long enough to settle a score with Charlie White, a bartender on the southeast corner of the Las Vegas plaza with whom he had had a previous altercation in Dodge City. With Holliday at the time was his girlfriend, a frontier prostitute known as Kate Bender but generally referred to as "Big Nosed Kate," for reasons said to be rather obvious.

Leaving Kate at a hotel near the railroad depot and proceeding west across the river to the plaza, Holliday entered the saloon and immediately opened fire on White, who was busy serving customers at their tables. Customers hit the floor as White ducked behind the bar, came up with a six-shooter, and began returning his assailant's fire at close range. When the smoke had cleared, White was lying motionless on the floor, and Holliday, assuming he had killed his man, picked up Kate at the hotel and resumed his journey to Tombstone, Arizona. White was merely stunned by a bullet that grazed his spine, however, and was up and about a few hours later.

Doc Holliday, best remembered as a participant in the Battle of the O.K. Corral at Tombstone in October, 1881, succumbed to tuberculosis at Glenwood Springs, Colorado, in 1887.

Hoodoo Brown

Hyman G. Neill, better known as Hoodoo Brown, was generally acknowledged to be the leader of the so-called Dodge City Gang that ruled East Las Vegas during the town's formative period. Little is known of his background. Said to have come from a "good family" in St. Louis, he became a railroad follower, drifting through Kansas and Colorado as a small-time gambler and confidence man, occasionally being arrested on such minor charges as vagrancy. He followed the railroad into Las Vegas, and with the support of other drifters, soon managed to get himself established on the ground floor.

Neill was elected justice of the peace when East Las Vegas, as yet unincorporated, was organized as Precinct 29. He also served as acting coroner, and took upon himself the responsibilities of both mayor and town council. He organized a police force, consisting principally of former Kansas gunfighters, and collected the money for their salaries from local merchants who wanted and needed protection.

A description of Hoodoo Brown and some of his Las Vegas activities was furnished to the *Chicago Times* by a Las Vegas correspondent in March 1880, shortly after Neill's hasty exit from the New Mexico community. The article said in part:

> *He has been in the western wilds for many years, and for a long time was one of the worst class of low gamblers. A recital of the many terrible affairs with which he has been connected in this country would make a whole book of horribles. When he came here, there was a great bustle and excitement with building houses and railroads, and the roughs and gamblers being the only idle ones, had things pretty much their own way, and elected him justice of the peace and coroner. He conducted his business in a fearless manner, and rather won the admiration of the citizens, although they always mistrusted him.*
>
> *The novel way in which he always opened court contains a little grim humor and illustrates how law reigned here a few months ago. He would seat himself and say, "Myself and partner will now open court," pointing to a large, double-barreled Winchester lying against the desk at his side.*
>
> *He is a tall, thin man, has light hair, small mustache, and a rakish look which is a terrible giveaway, and one would at once set him down as a desperate character, and a man to beware of.*

Gunmen, gamblers, and others of shadowy and questionable backgrounds who served on Hoodoo Brown's police force from time to time in various capacities included Joe Carson, David "Mysterious Dave" Mather, Dave Rudabaugh, John Joshua Webb, Jack Lyons, Dan Miller, Charles Jones, and Tom Pickett. They operated in a high-handed and often lawless manner, feeling safe in the assurance that any charges brought against them quickly would be dismissed by their employer.

Neill's right-hand man in Las Vegas was John "Dutchy" Schunderberger, a strapping young fellow who was handy with his fists. Dutchy served as Neill's chief clerk and bodyguard, and swept out the office in the mornings. Dutchy apparently was not a talkative soul—a characteristic he shared with Mysterious Dave—but he was a handy man to have around when trouble started. The *Las Vegas Optic,* on January 10, 1880, told how Dutchy had come to the rescue of two of Hoodoo Brown's policemen:

> *Last night Jack Lyons made an arrest of one of Montezuma's frail daughters, and two Mexicans came to her rescue and was about to get away with Jack. He whistled for Joe Carson to put in an appearance, but the Mexicans were about to prove too much for both of them, when Dutchy suddenly turned up and dispensed a little Dutch justice by striking out from the shoulder and letting one of the Ms. have it under the butt of the ear. Joe thinks the fellow is turning somersaults yet. The daughter languished in the cooler last night.*

Dutchy also was called upon to perform tasks requiring a little less brawn, as witness this item in the *Optic* on December 26, 1879:

> *Squire Neill spliced his first couple Christmas Eve. He stood Joe Carson and Dutchy up on the floor and practiced on them before starting for the house where the bride and*

*groom awaited him. Passers-by thought he was reading the
riot act to Joe and Dutchy. He has hoo-dooed them for life,
though.*

The *Las Vegas Gazette* provided another glimpse of Hoodoo Brown's character in this brief item published on November 1, 1879:

> *Thursday evening a young man named Marshall
> when settling his bill at the Parker house had a dispute
> with K.P. Brown and invited him outdoors. On getting out,
> Marshall drew a pistol and stuck it in Brown's face.
> Brown returned to the office but could not get a pistol. Later
> in the evening someone had Marshall arrested and taken
> before Justice Neill in the new town, who after hearing
> evidence complimented both parties on their good looks and
> genteel appearance and advised them to divide the cost,
> which done, the case was dismissed.*

It may have been one of Neill's policemen who was involved in a shooting spree outside a dance hall on the east side
of the West Las Vegas plaza on the evening of August 5, 1879,
in which John MacPherson, a former Las Vegas police chief,
was fatally wounded, and another man, Charles Slick, suffered
an arm wound. The *Gazette* published what it said was "the
usual supposition that Slick was shot by mistake for some other
man and the shooting of MacPherson was accidental," but
reported later that "a good many other stories have been
circulated and it is stated openly that the little policeman shot
MacPherson and in explanation said that MacPherson was
aiming to shoot him and shot Slick, and that he then shot

MacPherson." According to the newspaper the policeman, not identified by name, followed the wounded MacPherson into the Exchange Hotel saloon to finish him off, but was prevented from doing so by the bartender. MacPherson, who had been shot in the stomach, lingered until the morning of August 9.

The *Gazette* said that MacPherson, about forty and single and a former resident of Joplin, Missouri, had been chief of police in Las Vegas the previous winter, during which time he had managed to secure indictments against a number of men for minor offenses. Since then he had lived in Lincoln County, the newspaper said, and it was thought he had returned to Las Vegas to secure other indictments.

A few hours after MacPherson's death on August 9, New Mexico Chief Justice L. Bradford Prince of Santa Fe summoned Las Vegas police officers and deputy sheriffs before him in a Las Vegas courtroom and instructed them to strictly enforce the law against the carrying of deadly weapons, a law which he said was being openly violated. "Every difficulty that occurs in town grows out of a violation of this law, which should be strictly enforced, now that the influx of the population brought by the arrival of the railroad renders such difficulties particularly liable to occur," the chief justice said.

Five days later, on August 14, the *Optic* reported:

> Not so many killings to chronicle this week. Indeed, Las Vegas is a civil, law abiding but lively place. Life and limb are as safe here as anywhere on the globe; however, if you want a shooting match, just for the fun of the thing,

you needn't leave town for the purpose of hunting a cowboy.
You can be accommodated here.

The unidentified "little policeman" who shot MacPherson apparently skipped town.

W.F.M. Arny, former New Mexico acting governor and Indian agent, was among the victims of stagecoach robbers. (Courtesy Museum of New Mexico, negative 8789)

Stagecoach and Train Robberies

A masked man, seated on a log with a shotgun across his knees, waited patiently along the edge of the last remaining segment of the Santa Fe Trail about a dozen miles south of Las Vegas on the afternoon of August 18, 1879. At about 5 o'-clock a northbound stagecoach came in view, rumbling down a hillside, near the village of Tecolote. As the coach approached the seated figure, he calmly raised his shotgun and ordered the driver to halt. When the driver, Jack Davis, had pulled the horses to a stop, the masked man was joined by two companions, each masked and carrying a rifle. They politely ordered the two passengers in the coach to get out and sit down on the log.

The passengers were J.H. Strahan of New York, and William F.M. Arny of Santa Fe, a sixty-six-year-old former Virginia evangelist who since his arrival in New Mexico in 1861 had served variously as territorial secretary, acting governor, and Indian agent. Arny, a tall, bearded man with piercing eyes, refused to sit down, and as the *Weekly New Mexican* at Santa Fe reported a few days later, "perambulated around." Arny explained later that he walked around "for the purpose of noting what took place."

The leader of the robber trio ordered the man with the shotgun to keep Arny covered and make him stand still and asked his other companion to guard the driver and the other passenger while he went through the mail sacks. He then cut open the mail sacks with a knife, emptied their contents on the ground, and began tearing open the letters in search of currency. Arny, angered by this needless destruction of the mail, told the bandit leader to be more careful. He obeyed, carefully opening the end of each envelope.

When the mail had been opened and all valuable contents removed, the road agents turned their attention to the two passengers. Strahan was relieved of about $200 in cash. One of the robbers searched Arny twice without finding any money, and began to walk away from him.

"Go through that antediluvian gentleman again and this time find his money," the bandit leader ordered.

The robber then searched Arny a third time, and this time found his money and his watch. The watch was returned to him, however, when Arny pointed out that it had his name engraved on it. Arny grabbed for the bandit leader's gun, and during a brief scuffle, managed to unmask him for a moment.

The three robbers unhitched the horses from the stagecoach and rode off on them after warning the coach driver and his two passengers to remain where they were for at least twenty minutes. Their loot was estimated at from $400 to $500, plus Strahan's gold watch.

Two days after the robbery, three suspects were arrested in Las Vegas by G.W. Cole, a Santa Fe Railroad police officer who had been conferring with local authorities—presumably Hoodoo Brown and his staff. Taken into custody were

William Clancy, a railroad worker; Antonio López, described as "a tall, dark Chilean of bold appearance who could speak English," and Elijio Perea, described as a small Mexican with dark hair.

Charged with robbing the U.S. mails, the three were taken before U.S. Commissioner S.A. Hubbell for a preliminary hearing. At the hearing, Arny identified Clancy as the bandit leader he had unmasked briefly during the robbery. He said he recognized López by his voice, but that he could not identify Perea as one of the robbers. Perea was released, and Clancy and Lopez were taken to Santa Fe by U.S. Marshal John S. Morrison where they were placed in jail pending a grand jury investigation. James Dunnigan, charged with complicity in the coach robbery, was released from custody when he produced alibi witnesses who testified that he had been with them in Las Vegas during the afternoon and evening of the robbery.

It soon became rather obvious that Clancy and López had nothing to do with the robbery either, for a second stagecoach robbery occurred a few miles south of Las Vegas on the afternoon of August 30, and the driver, Jack Davis again, said that the robbers were the same men who had held up his coach on August 18, plus at least three others.

Passengers aboard this coach were identified by the *Las Vegas Gazette* as a Mrs. Abbott and her son of Prescott, Arizona; John H. Watts of Santa Fe; a Mr. Caldwell, member of a railroad survey party; Eugenio Romero, Las Vegas merchant and political leader; and Benjamin Stoop, a Las Vegas butcher. Also aboard the stage were John Forsha of Alamosa, Colorado, the express agent, and Charles Dudrow of Santa Fe, the express messenger.

The *Gazette* gave a detailed account of the robbery:

> *The place selected by the gentlemen of the road was the second Puertocito (small pass) between Las Vegas and Tecolote. This is a narrow gorge through which the road winds its way. It is extremely rocky and the hills rise up abruptly on either hand. The coach from Santa Fe passes this point near sundown. The robbers thus have plenty of daylight in which to make their examination of passengers, mail and express and escape when night closes down. In this case there were four robbers masked with a veil over their faces. They were only armed with Colt's 45 calibre pistols, a sufficiently formidable weapon for ordinary purposes. They suddenly appeared in the road and covered the driver with their pistols and ordered him to halt. They then ordered the passengers out of the coach and stood the men up in line. The driver, Jack Davis, was ordered to get down when one of the robbers mounted to the boot and drove the coach up a short distance. The large man of the robbers appeared to be the chief and directed all movements. The passengers were at first kept standing but were afterwards allowed to sit on a log. One robber with a brace of pistols was assigned guard duty over them. Mrs. Abbott, the only lady passenger, was seated opposite and could look back up the hill over them. She says two other men were seated on the rocks up the hill also with pistols covering the passengers. The mails were taken and thoroughly examined. There was likely some money found in the express and mail.*
>
> *The chief robber ordered one of his men, a small man, to examine the passengers. The latter rolled up his sleeves and went at it. Each passenger would stand in turn and*

take his medicine. We do not learn that they obtained much from the passengers. Travelers on the coaches are not in the habit of carrying much money with them, these times. They allowed each passenger 50 cts. to go get supper with. Stoop only had 15 cts. in change and requested they make up the difference to him. They politely informed him that he might go to h————! John H. Watts fortunately left his watch at home. They examined the messenger of the coach closely and even had him take off his boots. They obtained two watches but on learning that one was silver the chief ordered it be given back to the owner. On taking their departure the robbers ordered the passengers to remain 20 minutes before leaving the place. This injunction was not very closely observed, Mr. Romero starting to walk to his brother's home accompanied by Mr. Watts and several other passengers. They had proceeded but a short distance when a buggy came out of the woods to the left with a couple of men in it accompanied by several men riding the stage horses. They all traveled on in the direction of town. We learn that a couple of men had obtained a buggy at Parker's corral in the afternoon and his buggy came back directly after the robbery, the horses covered with sweat. The men after paying for the buggy quietly disappeared and have not been seen since. This would indicate that they had gone out in a buggy to rob the coach. That is evidently an aristocratic business.

As in the preceding robbery, the bandits departed from the scene with horses taken from the stagecoach. Forsha, the express agent, walking toward Las Vegas from the stranded coach, found a mare on the trail, mounted it, and rode quickly into Las Vegas to report the robbery. He said the robbers probably arrived in town only five minutes ahead of him.

The *Gazette* expressed the belief on September 4 that the latest turn of events established the innocence of Clancy and López:

> *The New Mexican says that the men who were arrested two weeks ago for robbing the stage are safely confined in jail in Santa Fe, but stage robbing goes on, and the driver, who ought to be posted, says that the same men did the work both times. It will be rather hard on the boys to have to lay in jail till November, and then on trial be found not guilty.*

The next day, the *Gazette* told of the precautions that were being taken by the railroad against road agents:

> *All the employees on the train from La Junta to Las Vegas have been furnished with carbines and ammunition to protect the passengers and express from road agents. Men who know how to shoot, and are experienced in the use of Winchester rifles at short range are being placed on the train. It is not probable the order to "hold up your hands" will be obeyed under any circumstances.*

Charles Adams, a Post Office Department detective, arrived in Las Vegas by train from Denver on the morning of September 11, conferred with some of the local law enforcement officials during the day, and that night arrested three suspects in connection with the second stagecoach robbery on August 30. Arrested while dealing keno in the Centre Street saloon he operated in partnership with Doc Holliday was Jordan L. Webb, identified as one of the men who had hired a buggy at Parker's corral on the afternoon of the robbery. Also arrested in the saloon were two gamblers, William Nicholson—alias "Slap Jack Bill, the Pride of the Panhandle" —and John Pierce, alias "Bull Shit Jack," railroad followers who had drifted into town several weeks before. The U.S. marshal escorted the three to jail in Santa Fe the next day to face federal charges of robbing the U.S. mails. They were soon joined in jail by a fourth suspect, Frank Cady.

With six accused mail robbers in jail, railroad officials apparently relaxed their vigilance, for a train was held up and robbed on the night of October 14 just outside of Las Vegas, and the order to "hold up your hands" apparently was obeyed without resistance. Meager details of the robbery were reported in the *New Mexican* on Saturday, October 18:

> *Last Tuesday night the east bound train on the A.T. & S.F. R.R. was stopped and robbed by two armed men about half a mile from Las Vegas, in a deep cut. The passengers were not disturbed, but the messenger in charge of the express box was relieved of $90, the property of the express company.*

Other newspaper reports later indicated that four or five robbers had entered the express and baggage car shortly after the train had pulled north out of the depot, held up the express messenger, took $1,000 or $2,000 in cash and about the same amount in drafts from the express box, jumped out of the moving train, and walked back to town. Arrested and jailed in Las Vegas in connection with the train robbery were three men, Joseph and William Stokes, who were brothers, and William Mullen, alias "The Pock-Marked Kid."

Mystery, meanwhile, continued to surround the coach and train robberies, with a number of Las Vegas citizens, including policemen, accused of complicity in the robberies or of being accessories. Several of these cases were disposed of in the court of Justice of the Peace Arthur Morrison in West Las Vegas on November 3, 1879. David Rudabaugh and Joseph Martin, who had been accused in connection with the stage robberies, entered pleas of not guilty and were released for lack of prosecution and evidence. Mysterious Dave Mather, accused of being an accessory in the train robbery, also pleaded not guilty and was released for lack of prosecution.

The *Optic,* happy that Mather, the East Las Vegas policeman, had been exonerated, reported on November 5: "We are glad to learn that David A. Mathre (cq) has been exonerated from all complicity in the recent robbery of the train. Everybody knew this as his recent arrest was only a little piece of malice upon the part of another." The newspapers indicated that the malice against Mysterious Dave was borne by one Frank P. "Texas Frank" Whitfield, but for reasons not given.

The charges against Rudabaugh and Martin apparently were lodged by G.W. Cole, the railroad detective who earlier had arrested Clancy, López, and Perea for the crime. After leaving New Mexico in the fall of 1879, the detective was quoted in the newspapers as claiming that Dave Rudabaugh, who had been involved in an attempted train robbery in Kansas in 1878, was now the leader of a band of robbers in New Mexico. The *Optic* defended Rudabaugh on December 26, 1879, saying:

For some time he has been in charge of a stage route from Otero, New Mexico, to Camp Supply, Indian Territory, a distance of three hundred and sixty miles, and has gained the confidence of his employers and the public by his energy and honesty.

And besides, by that time, Detective Cole had been arrested in Dallas, Texas, on a charge of making and passing counterfeit money. An alleged accessory, identified as Mrs. Page, alias McCrary, had been arrested in Denver, Colorado, where she was operating a saloon.

Most of those arrested in connection with the stagecoach and train robberies were to languish in the Santa Fe jail for more than a year before their innocence was established.

The Goddess of Chance

A beautiful, dark-eyed brunette arrived in East Las Vegas in September 1879, and began dealing faro and monte in the Toe Jam Saloon on Centre Street near the railroad.

She called herself Monte Verde, although Las Vegas newspapers usually referred to her as Monte Holman, since she worked in partnership with Eugene Holman, who was described by the newspapers as her "heavy man." The fact that she was the mother or guardian of a child was indicated in one brief newspaper item mentioning that a man had ravished "Monte Holman's little girl."

Monte Verde was about forty years of age when she reached Las Vegas, and it was said that her beauty remained intact despite years of dissipation that included drug and alcohol abuse and at least one suicide attempt. She attracted a great deal of attention during the months she spent in Las Vegas as a card dealer and entertainer. Her favorite costumes were of red or black velvet, decorated gaudily with diamonds and rubies. Gold and diamond clasps were fastened to her luxuriant black hair, which hung carelessly over her shoulders.

Pale, stern, and impassive, never showing a spark of

human kindness, Monte Verde provided a bit of mysterious glamour in the often sordid saloons and gambling halls in which she plied her trade. She hated every man who played against her, showing no remorse or pity when she took the last cent of a cowboy or railroad man. She despised all women, and seldom spoke to them or of them. She never quarreled. Her will was the law, which she enforced merely by picking up her revolver. She never spoke of her past, and few if any in Las Vegas knew the remarkable story of her background.

She left Las Vegas in the winter of 1879–1880, seeking greener pastures in El Paso, Texas, and Tombstone, Arizona, but returned to Las Vegas in March 1880 to open a "palace of pleasure" known as The Parlor. During the months that followed she also appeared as a variety actress and vaudeville entertainer at the Globe Theater in East Las Vegas. That summer she persuaded a Las Vegas citizen to build her her own theater, where she appeared until it was destroyed by fire in September 1880.

Soon afterwards, she and Eugene Holman left Las Vegas, traveling north into Colorado. She never returned. It was a year after her departure that the facts of her remarkable life became known to citizens of the New Mexico community.

The *Las Vegas Optic,* on October 18, 1881, reprinted a lengthy story about the life of Monte Verde that had been published a short while before in a San Francisco newspaper. The California newspaper said that Monte Verde was dying in a San Francisco hospital after being found near death in a Chinese opium den. The article revealed that Monte Verde was Belle Siddons, a former Missouri socialite who had been a notorious Confederate spy during the Civil War.

Belle Siddons had been attending the Missouri Female

Seminary at Lexington, Missouri, shortly before the Civil War when her uncle, Claiborne Fox Jackson, was elected governor of the state. Upon her graduation, she went to the capital at Jefferson City, made her debut in society, and became an immediate sensation because of her charms and remarkable beauty. Politicians and legislators of all ages vied for her affections, but she gave her heart to a prominent newspaperman who was engaged to another woman. The journalist had not sought her love and was slow to reciprocate, but eventually succumbed to her charms and became her devoted worshiper.

The Civil War flamed and the journalist went off to war, only to be killed in battle. Belle was grief stricken, but gave no outward display of her emotions. Instead, she became the gayest of the gay, the belle of St. Louis, dining, dancing, riding, and attending performances at the opera house with officers of the Union Army. In December 1862, it was found that she was furnishing information she had obtained from her Union officer friends to two Confederate generals, Nathan Bedford Forrest and Sterling Price—information which, among other things, had enabled the Confederates to thwart Gen. U.S. Grant's attempts to cut the Memphis and Mobile Railroad. Arrested and placed in a prison for rebels in St. Louis, she was released after four months on condition that she leave the state for the duration of the war. She spent the remainder of the war in southern states.

After the war she reappeared at the Missouri capital, this time as a lobbyist. She became notorious for the subtle power and influence she had over certain members of the state legislature, and scandalous stories were told about her.

In 1868 she met and married Dr. Newt Hallet, a Kansas City physician and inveterate gambler, and the two went to

Houston and Fort Brown, Texas. Dr. Hallet died in a yellow-fever epidemic in Texas in 1869. His widow apparently had learned some of his gambling skills during their brief marriage, for a few months after his death she was dealing monte and black jack in New Orleans. Taking the name Madame Vestal, she started out on her own, setting up gaming tables in the Kansas cowtowns of Wichita and Ellsworth and gradually moving west to Cheyenne, Wyoming, and Denver, Colorado.

When the Black Hills gold rush started in 1876, she bought an expensive four-horse carriage in Denver, had it remodeled into an elaborate boudoir, and headed overland to Deadwood with tents and gambling equipment. In Deadwood she took the name Lurline Monte Verde and set up a gambling establishment in a large tent on the main street of the town.

In Deadwood she met and fell in love with Archie McLaughlin, also known as Archie Cummings, a leader of a band of road agents who had served as a Confederate guerrilla fighter under William C. Quantrill in Kansas during the early years of the Civil War. Soon, it was said, she was plotting every move the gang made. After an abortive attempt to hold up a stagecoach outside Deadwood on July 2, 1878, in which one member of the gang was killed and another wounded, McLaughlin and two companions fled west to a secret hideout in Wyoming.

A handsome detective, Boone May, managed to win Monte Verde's confidence and learned from her the hiding place of her lover, and McLaughlin and his two companions were captured north of Cheyenne. As the three were being returned to Deadwood on a stagecoach, a group of vigilantes stopped the coach north of Fort Laramie on November 3, took the prisoners from the coach, and hanged them from some nearby cottonwood trees.

When she learned of McLaughlin's fate, the heart-broken lady gambler sent for a newspaper reporter, dictated her obituary, and drank poison. She survived the suicide attempt, however, and moved to Leadville, Colorado, where she operated a music hall and dance house. Leaving Leadville in 1879, she moved south into New Mexico, stopping at Las Vegas.

The *Optic*, when reprinting the San Francisco article in 1881, recalled Monte Verde's stay in Las Vegas:

> *The doings of Monte Verde, as she was known here, while she sojourned among us, would fill a volume. She came to Las Vegas in September, 1879, and dealt "short faro" in the "Toe-Jam" saloon on Centre Street, where the Bon Ton saloon now stands. There she led a life of dissipation, and shortly afterwards appeared at the Globe theatre, where McDonald's whiskey store has been located, as a leading variety lady. Her banjo solos will be remembered by all the old boys of the town, and "their memory will steel o'er," etc. She went to the lower country and returned in March, 1880, and opened "the Parlor," a palace of pleasure, on Sixth street. She again entered a variety theater, and was the "heavy gal" in a Railroad avenue vaudeville. She had a citizen build a theater on Centre street, and played in it until the fire of September, 1880. During her residence in Las Vegas she wrote several effusions of poetry to The Optic, and was a great friend of journalists, courting their favors on every occasion. She has ruined many a Las Vegas young man, and "broke up" some of the older ones, a number of whom still reside here. With 'Gene*

Holman, her solid man, she left Las Vegas a year ago, and went to Colorado, and from thence to California, as stated by the Frisco reporter. No one in Las Vegas knew her full history, and the foregoing romance will be received here with great interest.

As for her writing "several effusions of poetry to The Optic," Monte Verde might well have been the author of an unsigned poem entitled "Wild Flowers," which was published in the newspaper on May 21, 1880, during her residence in Las Vegas. It said, in part:

Alas, my childhood and my blossoms faded, And I, in stranger lands have wandered far; My buoyance is gone; I'm worn and jaded, And blighting sorrow came my joy to mar.

The Dance Hall Battle

Four cowboy desperadoes, bent on having a good time, seeing the sights, and letting off a little steam, arrived in Las Vegas one day in January 1880 and began making the rounds of the saloons, gambling halls, and places of ill repute. The four, according to *The Optic,* paraded the streets armed to the teeth and laughed at law officers who suggested that they check their weapons until they were ready to leave town.

The leader of the group, who called himself Tom Henry, was a twenty-one-year-old cowboy who reportedly had a "checkered career" in Texas. His companions were known as John Dorsey, James West, and William Randall. The group reportedly had come to the region to steal horses.

On the night of January 22, after several days of making a general nuisance of themselves, flouting law officers, and becoming drunker by the hour, the four entered the crowded Close and Patterson dance hall in East Las Vegas, armed with their pistols.

Joe Carson, the forty-year-old town marshal, approached the cowboys and asked them to check their guns. They laughed in his face. Carson repeated his request, and the answer was a barrage of profane insults which suddenly became a barrage of bullets. The cowboys drew their guns and opened fire on the marshal, who managed to pull his gun from his hip pocket and fire two shots before falling to the floor with nine bullets in his body.

David "Mysterious Dave" Mather, assistant town marshal, who was standing nearby, drew his revolver and opened fire on the cowboys. It was estimated that forty shots were fired in the dance hall during the battle. When the smoke had cleared, it was found that one of the cowboys, William Randall, was dead on the floor, as was Marshal Carson. Another of the cowboys, James West, was down with a bullet through his middle, but still alive.

Tom Henry, shot in the calf of his leg, escaped out the door and limped to the Lewelling and Olds Corral, where at gunpoint he ordered an employee of the corral to begin saddling up horses. He didn't know at the moment how many horses would be needed, for he wasn't sure how many of his companions were in a condition to join him. Henry was joined at the corral in a moment by John Dorsey, who had escaped unharmed. The two rode out of town at a gallop, Henry threatening to "wreak vengeance on the damned town by laying it in ashes," according to newspaper reports. James West, the wounded man left behind, was hauled off to jail.

The *Optic,* on January 24, told of a visit to the slain marshal's widow:

> *Today we visited Mrs. Carson, who is heart-broken and disconsolate over the brutal murder of her husband. She has his garments, which are perforated with bullet holes, carefully folded away in her trunk. There are eight*

*bullet holes in his coat, and one in his boot, showing that
he was shot nine times. The badges worn by Joe, as well as
his rings, pocket knife, money—in fact everything he had
on his person that bloody night, with a lock of his hair,
have been carefully laid aside and many times will she weep
over them. . . .*

*On the night he met his death, Joe had two revolvers
on his person—one in a scabbard around his body and one
in his hip pocket. The chambers in the latter one were empty
and, as traces of blood are visible, it is thought that poor
Joe managed to get it out of his pocket and fire two shots at
his assailants. . . .*

The newspaper added that the Carsons were the parents of a
fourteen-year-old daughter who was attending school in Nash-
ville, Tennessee. The marshal's father was living near Rome,
Georgia, the article continued, and Mrs. Carson planned to
return to the home of her parents in Chicago after the funeral
of her husband.

The *Optic,* in the same issue, opined that Mysterious
Dave, who had come through the battle unharmed, was bulletproof: "Dave Mather is bullet proof. A ball passed through
both coats he had on at the shooting affair Thursday night."

About two weeks later, the proprietors of the Lewelling
and Olds Corral learned that the two horses that had been
appropriated at the corral by the cowboys who were escaping
had been seen to the north in Mora County. Charles Olds and
Harry Combs rode to Mora, which was the county seat, about
thirty miles to the north, and then returned to Las Vegas on
February 2 with the recovered horses and with word that
Henry and Dorsey were hiding out in a farmhouse near Mora,

waiting for Henry's leg wound to heal before hightailing it out of the country.

A group of heavily armed East Las Vegas lawmen and deputies climbed into a wagon on the afternoon of February 5 and started for Mora. The posse, according to *The Optic,* included J.J. Webb, William L. Goodlet, Bill Combs, Dave Rudabaugh, Lee Smith, and a man identified only as Muldoon. Most or all of them were considered members of Hoodoo Brown's Dodge City Gang.

Arriving in Mora that night, the posse spent its duration in Thomas Walton's hotel. Rising early the next morning, they proceeded to the farmhouse where the two fugitives were believed to be hiding. The Las Vegas group was accompanied to the farm by A.P. Branch, sheriff of Mora County, and John Daugherty, a local rancher.

The posse reached and took up positions around the farmhouse at about 10 a.m. (on February 6) and called upon the fugitives to surrender. Henry, whom *The Optic* said "would rather fight than eat," refused to surrender and prepared to defend himself. His companion, Dorsey, persuaded him to give up without a fight, however, and the two agreed to surrender on condition that they would be protected from any mob violence in Las Vegas. The posse, with its two prisoners in a wagon, reached Las Vegas that afternoon and the two were subsequently placed in jail with their wounded companion, West.

Henry and Dorsey had been reluctant to talk about the dance-hall shootings with their captors during the ride to Las Vegas. *The Optic* reported on February 7 that Henry had made the only reference to the "fatal fuss" and attributed the whole difficulty to whiskey, adding:

> *However, in speaking of this lamentable affair, his demeanor all the time was unruffled and nonchalant, as if he were the guest of the party instead of a man under arrest for a foul, cowardly murder for which he may be "jerked to Jesus" before the sun rises again.*

Interviewed at the jail by an *Optic* reporter, Henry said he was drunk at the time of the dance-hall battle and did not know what he was doing. The article added:

> *He remarked, further, that when a fellow of his disposition got too much whiskey on board, he lost control of himself and was driven to deeds, the enormity of which were not realized until more sober moments.*

The *Optic*'s prediction on February 7 that Henry would be "jerked to Jesus before the sun rises again" proved to be accurate. That night, about 100 Las Vegas citizens gathered silently in the streets and marched to the jail. They battered down the door, demanded and received the keys to the cells from the jailer, opened cell doors, and led Henry and Dorsey out with ropes around their necks. The wounded West was carried from his cell.

Leading and carrying the prisoners through the dark streets to the West Las Vegas Plaza, the mob halted at the windmill in the center of the plaza—the "hanging windmill"—and dragged the three up to the windmill platform, the ropes still around their necks. The nooses were adjusted, and the other ends of the ropes looped up over beams in the windmill superstructure.

The three were asked if they had anything to say before

being hanged. Tom Henry replied that his true name was Thomas Jefferson House, and requested that somebody write to his parents, Mr. and Mrs. U.B. House, in Pueblo, Colorado.

"Boys, it's pretty rough to be hung, but I wish some one would write to my father and mother," he said. "I will stand the consequence and die like a man."

James West said only that his real name was James Lowe, although it was determined later that he was Anthony Lowe, from Kansas. James Dorsey would say nothing of his background, declaring that he had not a friend or a relative in the world.

West, suffering from his wounds and shivering in the cold, was selected to be the first to pay the penalty. When he began to whimper, Henry turned to him and said, "Jim, be still and die like a man."

"Boys, you are hanging a mighty good man," West said, regaining his composure. His last words before he was swung into the air were, "Please button up my pants."

At that moment, according to some of the reports, Joe Carson's widow, who was in the crowd, picked up a rifle and began shooting at the three victims. General gunfire then erupted as the mob followed her lead. Tom Henry, falling to his knees in the ensuing hail of bullets, crawled to the edge of the windmill platform, pleading: "Boys, for God's sake shoot me again; shoot me in the head." In a moment, all three were dead in pools of blood on the windmill platform. Each man later was placed in a coffin, and the three were buried in a single grave.

The *Optic,* on February 9, published the verdict of the West Las Vegas coroner's jury:

We, the justice of the peace and jury, who sat upon the inquest held this day, Feb. 8, 1880, on the body of three men whose names are Tom Henry, John Dorsey and James West, found on the public plaza, find that the two former persons came to death by several shots in their heads, and the latter one by signs of being hanged by the neck by some person or persons unknown, at about 2 or 3 o'clock in the morning on the day as above stated. We also found that the doors of the jail were broken open and from investigation we learn that the above men were taken out of their cells by a mob, unknown to this jury. (Signed) Arthur Morrison, J.P., Charles Ilfeld, M. Whiteman, Theodosio Lucero, H. Romero, Antonio José Baca, J. Felipe Baca.

Another brief item in the *Optic* the same day said: "There is a petition in circulation to have the windmill torn down. It is too great a temptation." The "hanging windmill" was torn down that same day, not only because it was a great temptation but also because it was a bad influence on the children of Las Vegas. As *The Las Vegas Gazette* reported on February 10:

The windpump in the plaza by the repeated tragedies exacted thereon became of such bad memory that the citizens determined that it should come down, and a purse was raised and a carpenter sent to work yesterday who took down the scaffold close to the foundation. The bad effects of such sights on children cannot be realized. Yesterday boys were hanging dogs all over town and many a poor dog had his neck stretched just by force of example.

Mysterious Dave

With the death of Joe Carson, Hoodoo Brown's town marshal, the job passed to Carson's "bulletproof" assistant, David "Mysterious Dave" Mather, another member of the Dodge City Gang. Described as a medium-sized, rather handsome man with black, piercing eyes and a black, drooping mustache, Mather was a man of mystery in every sense of the word. Quiet, stealthy, and dangerous, a man with whom it was difficult to make friends, he was a phantom figure of the Las Vegas scene.

Las Vegas newspapers, as well as other newspapers and official documents, were never quite sure of his name, giving his surname variously as Mather, Mathre, Mathers, and Matthews, and his middle initial as both A and H. Practically nothing is known of the first quarter-century of his life or of his later years and eventual fate. Kansas census records indicate that he was born in Connecticut in 1845. He claimed, according to at least one newspaper report, that he was a lineal descendant of Cotton Mather, the early New England Puritan minister, philosopher, and author noted for his involvement in the Salem witchcraft trials.

David "Mysterious Dave" Mather, Las Vegas town marshal and alleged train robber. (Courtesy Kansas State Historical Society, Topeka)

Dave Mather was about thirty years old when he first appeared in Dodge City in the mid-1870s. Before that, it was said, he had spent several years as a member of a cattle-rustling gang in Arkansas and as a buffalo hunter on the Texas plains. He took up gambling in the Kansas cow town, and almost died when he was slashed across the stomach with a knife during a gambling dispute. In 1878, he and part-time lawman Wyatt Earp were chased out of Mobeetie, Texas, where they had been peddling phony gold bricks to naive citizens, claiming the bricks came from a long lost Spanish gold mine. Mather also was reported to have killed a man in Mobeetie.

Mysterious Dave joined the exodus of Kansas desperadoes to Las Vegas in the summer of 1879 and quickly became identified with Hoodoo Brown's Dodge City Gang as a member of the peace justice's merchant police force. San Miguel County records show that he was appointed constable of Precinct 29, East Las Vegas, on August 20, 1879, succeeding Simón Padilla Soto, who had resigned. It was while he was serving as a lawman that he was charged with being an accessory in the train robbery outside Las Vegas on October 14, 1879, and was released for lack of prosecution.

A month later, the *Las Vegas Gazette* took him to task for "promiscuous shooting" in connection with a row involving some soldiers. The *Gazette,* which referred to Mather as "Mr. Matthews," reported on November 22, 1879:

> *Night before last, while the soldiers were stationed in town, several of the boys went over to the new town and imbibed a little too much benzine and consequently became noisy and boistrous. They were arrested by the officers of the new town, loaded into one of Hutchinson and Company's*

hacks and started for the jail. One of them, however, broke away and started to run. Mr. Matthews ordered him to halt, but he refused to obey, whereupon he was pursued and fired at some five or six times, one of the shots taking effect in the thumb. He was then taken and lodged in jail. The duty of an officer is a delicate one and should be criticized as little as possible. Yet the offense committed by the soldiers seems to be rather too small a one to justify such promiscous shooting. Not only was the life of the offender in danger but also the lives of those on the streets, and even the houses in the immediate vicinity. Officers as well as others should be careful about the use of firearms.

The doings of Mysterious Dave mystified the *Las Vegas Optic* during the next several months with some rather vague items that would indicate that Mather's authority and jurisdiction exceeded that of a town constable. Said the *Optic* on December 1, 1879: "Dave Mather left for Wichita, Kansas, last night in response to a telegram requesting him to apprehend two or three villainously-inclined gentlemen."

Mather didn't remain in Kansas very long, because an item in the *Optic* on December 17 revealed that he was off on yet another mysterious journey: "Mysterious Dave Mathers left by mule team for Fort Stanton this morning. He goes on 'official business,' the meaning of which no man can fathom." Then, on December 31, the newspaper said that: "Mysterious Dave has returned from Fort Stanton and is now menaced with a trip to Fort Sumner." Mather's departure for Fort Sumner was noted by the newspaper on January 2, 1880: "Mysterious Dave, J.J. Webb and Charley Coombs started for Fort Sumner yesterday, in buggies from Hutchinson & Co.'s stable. Their business will be made known upon their return."

Their business was not made known upon their return, however, although one of the three apparently furnished the newspaper with a few details of the trip. Under a headline reading "They Have Returned," the *Optic* reported on January 8:

> *Mysterious Dave, Webb and Combs left here a few days ago for the vicinity of Fort Sumner for some one that the law was reaching out for with its strong right arm. When the boys arrived within some ten miles of Sumner, they were met by a crowd of big burley fellows, each armed with a Winchester rifle and a couple of six shooters, and informed that they were known and that no minions of the law were wanted in that country; that they had better about face and take the back trail for Vegas; that they need not stand on the order of going but go at once. The boys held a short council and considering discretion the better part of valor turned their horses' heads toward the setting of the sun, and soon found themselves at home. Dave says he has lost no one, either in that part of the country or in Lincoln county.*

Three nights after the East Las Vegas dance-hall battle, during which Mather was credited with killing William Randall and wounding James West and Tom Henry, Mysterious Dave shot down a young railroad worker in front of an East Las Vegas restaurant. The *Optic,* on the following day, told the story under a headline reading: "A Wrong Play. Joe Castello Pulls His Pistol on Dave Mather and is Killed. An Unfortunate Affair."

Castello, a railroad telegrapher, had arrived in Las Vegas on the morning of January 25, 1880, with a squad of men from Kansas who were on their way south to help build the Santa Fe Railroad line. The railroad workers visited the saloons that afternoon, indulged quite freely, and became rather quarrelsome. Castello, a twenty-two-year-old St. Louis resident, remained sober and tried to keep some semblance of order among the men.

That night, between 10 and 11 p.m., two of the railroad workers began fighting in front of McKay's restaurant, and Castello intervened in an effort to stop the trouble. A large crowd gathered quickly at the scene of the disturbance, and Castello drew his pistol and asked them to leave. One of the railroad workers also drew a pistol. The *Optic* told what happened next:

> At this juncture Dave Mather appeared on the scene and commanded the parties to put up their weapons as we had had trouble enough of late. Instead of complying with the request, Castello suddenly pointed his murderous weapon at Dave Mather, and with a cocked pistol in his hand, threatened to shoot the officer if he advanced another step. Dave knew his duty and knew the consequences that would result from a delay of action, so he advanced and, in a twinkling of an eye, almost before the breathless bystanders had time to see a movement on his part, he drew his trusty revolver from its place and fired one shot at the determined man, the ball taking effect in Castello's left side below the ribs, penetrating the lung, and ranging downward, through the stomach and liver. Of course the man could not live.

Castello, mortally wounded, was carried into Hoodoo Brown's office, and a physician, Dr. Russell Bayly, was summoned. The doctor remained with Castello until 6 the following morning, January 26, when the telegrapher breathed his last.

A coroner's jury, convened that day by H.G. Neill (Hoodoo Brown), found that Joseph Castello "came to his death by a pistol shot fired from a pistol in the hands of D.H. Mather, constable, in the discharge of his duties as an officer; and that said shooting was justifiable, and in self protection." The verdict was signed by E.G. Arment, W.H. Bennett, William L. Goodlett, E.W. Sebben, William N. Moran, M.S. Bradley, and H.G. Neill, acting coroner.

Following the dance-hall battle, Mather was identified by the newspapers variously as town marshal and as constable. The *Optic* reported two days after Joe Carson's death that Mather had appointed (J.J.) Webb and Pfleiger as his assistants, to work as night patrolmen. Mather apparently appointed Dave Rudabaugh as an assistant, too, for the *Optic* on February 21 noted that Mather and Rudabaugh had arrested a suspect in the burglary of Phillip Holzman's store and had taken him before Hoodoo Brown, who had bound him over to jail.

The newspapers said that Mather, Hoodoo Brown, and several other Las Vegas residents were in Santa Fe during the last week in February to testify at the trial of Jordan L. Webb, the Las Vegas saloon keeper charged in connection with the August stagecoach robberies. The jury, on February 28, failed to agree on a verdict.

Mather resigned his position upon his return to Las Vegas. The *Optic* reported on March 3, 1880:

*Dave Mather has resigned his position as town mar-
shal and J.J. Webb will no longer serve as an officer, owing
to the inadequacy of the pay received for performing the
duties assigned to them. An officer who does his duty should
be paid promptly and well. No man can afford to work for
nothing, particularly at the risk of his life.*

Mather returned to Dodge City, took up gambling again,
but didn't stay there long. During the remainder of 1880 he
reportedly was seen at various places in Colorado and Texas.
Early in 1881 he was jailed in San Antonio, Texas, on a charge
of passing counterfeit money, but he apparently escaped any
serious consequences, for later in the year he was employed
as an assistant town marshal at El Paso, Texas. Here, again, he
resigned the post because of the inadequacy of the pay.

Dallas was his next stop, and there he became intimately
involved with Georgia Morgan, a black (or mulatto) madam
of a popular sporting house. In January 1882, he stole a gold
chain and ring from her and hurried west to Fort Worth. She
followed him there with a knife and gun, creating such an
uproar when she found him that she was arrested and fined for
disturbing the peace.

On March 29, 1883, J.C. Martin of Travis County, Texas,
wrote to the governor of Kansas asking if there was a reward
offered by his state for "a desperado and gambler who goes
under the name of Mysterious Dave," saying that he heard he
was wanted in Kansas for murder, and that he could get him
at any time. Gov. G.W. Click answered that he had no information on the subject.

Returning once again to Dodge City, Mather served as an
assistant town marshal and deputy sheriff in 1883 and 1884,

and operated the Mather & Black dance hall in the opera house. After his dance-hall license was suspended, he operated a saloon on the second floor of the opera house. When the town administration changed in February 1884, Mather lost his job as assistant town marshal and was replaced by Tom Nixon, a long-time Dodge City resident and former buffalo hunter. Mather kept his job as deputy sheriff, however.

Mather was standing at the head of the opera-house stairway on the night of July 18, 1884, when Nixon appeared at the foot of the stairway, fired one shot at him, and disappeared in the darkness. The bullet missed its mark, splintering some woodwork next to Mather and sending a splinter into the little finger of Mather's left hand. Newspapers said the incident was the result of an old feud between Mather and Nixon. Reports circulated that Mather blamed Nixon for suspending his dance-hall license, and that Nixon thought Mather was being overly attentive to Mrs. Nixon, an invalid with two children. Mather declined to press charges against Nixon, for reasons that soon became obvious.

Descending the stairway from his saloon three nights later, Mather saw Nixon standing nearby on a corner. When he reached the foot of the stairway, he called to Nixon by name, and then fired four bullets into his body, killing him instantly. Mather was acquitted of a murder charge on December 30, a jury in Kinsley, Kansas, finding that Nixon was the aggressor.

Mysterious Dave was joined in Dodge City by a brother, identified variously as Josiah Mather and Cyrus Mather, and both were charged with murder as the result of a gun battle in the Junction Saloon on May 10, 1885. Witnesses said that Mather and David Barnes, who sold groceries from his house, had been playing cards in the saloon when an argument erupted over some money. Mather struck Barnes, who was armed, a bullet went through Mather's hat, grazing his forehead, and an estimated dozen shots were fired in the next ten seconds, Josiah (or Cyrus) shooting from behind the bar. When the shooting was over, Barnes was dead and two bystanders wounded. The Mather brothers were released on $3,000 bonds, and never showed up for their trial.

Later, it was reported that Dave Mather was a lawman at New Kiowa, Kansas, and in 1887 he reportedly was living alone in a cabin near Long Pine, Nebraska, spending much of his time hunting game. He left Long Pine in 1888, telling friends he was heading south for a warmer climate, and here Mysterious Dave vanished from the pages of history.

The End of Gang Rule

Although Mysterious Dave Mather and John Joshua Webb gave inadequate pay as the reason for their leaving Hoodoo Brown's police force, the *Las Vegas Optic* reported on March 3, 1880, that it was the impending collapse of the Dodge City Gang and possible murder indictments that most influenced their hasty decisions.

The demise of the gang of desperadoes that had ruled East Las Vegas since the coming of the railroad was brought about by the unprovoked killing of Michael Kelliher in an East Las Vegas saloon during the early morning hours of March 2. Kelliher, a twenty-eight-year-old freighter, rancher, and former Chicago policeman, arrived in Las Vegas on Sunday night, February 29, his pants pocket bulging with a wad of more than $2,000 in currency. He was the owner of three freight teams, and with his brother, Morris Kelliher of Cheyenne, Wyoming, owned a ranch in the Dakotas. Michael had traveled south into New Mexico from Deadwood with the money to buy cattle.

While camped on the trail, a day out of Las Vegas, Kelliher had taken the money from his pants pocket and counted

147

it in front of his traveling companion, William Brickley. The count came to $2,115. Kelliher told Brickley that he would deposit most of it in a bank as soon as they reached Las Vegas.

Upon reaching Las Vegas on Sunday night, the two camped at the edge of town. Kelliher had no opportunity to deposit the money in a bank on Monday, however, for he spent the entire day trailing some horses that had strayed off from his camp that morning and had headed back north up the trail.

Kelliher returned to camp with the horses at sundown. He and Brickley cooked and ate their supper, then walked into town to see the sights and enjoy some of the night life. They visited a dance hall in West Las Vegas, then crossed the bridge to East Las Vegas and made the rounds of the dance halls and saloons in the new town. The fact that Kelliher carried a large sum of money in his pocket did not go unnoticed.

Returning to their camp at about 3 o'clock in the morning, the two stopped for a final drink at the Goodlet and Roberts Saloon, a favorite hangout for Hoodoo Brown, Dutchy, and others of the Dodge City Gang. They met an acquaintance in the saloon, and had been there from thirty to forty-five minutes when Officer J.J. Webb walked in and shot Kelliher dead.

H.G. Neill (Hoodoo Brown) arrived quickly on the scene and impaneled a coroner's jury of his friends in his capacity as acting coroner. The jury ruled that "the deceased came to his death from a pistol in the hands of J.J. Webb, being an officer in the discharge of his duty, and the killing was justifiable and necessary under the circumstances."

What were the circumstances? Witnesses, including

William Goodlet, one of the proprietors of the saloon, who was known to work hand-in-glove with the Dodge City Gang, testified that Kelliher was drunk and boisterous, had threatened to kill a policeman, was singing songs, and at one point had asked the bartender if he had any warclubs, saying he wanted to show how he could use them. The witnesses said Webb entered the saloon, asked Kelliher for his gun, and then shot him when Kelliher jumped back and placed his hand on his pistol.

This testimony was in conflict with the testimony given by Brickley, Kelliher's companion, who was described as being a large, red-complected man with blue eyes and a slight brogue. Brickley said that Kelliher had not threatened anybody, but was leaning on his elbow on the bar when Webb walked in, ordered him to throw up his hands, and immediately shot him to death.

A few hours after the shooting, Hoodoo Brown went to Charles Blanchard, San Miguel County probate judge, and asked permission to serve as administrator of Kelliher's estate. The justice of the peace and acting coroner said that he had taken $1,090 from the body of the deceased during the inquest at the saloon. A question of bond arose, and Blanchard said he would think about the matter. While he was thinking, it was brought to light that Hoodoo had taken $860 more from the dead man's pocket than he had reported.

A grand jury, which was in session in the courthouse in West Las Vegas at the time, investigated the Kelliher shooting and heard evidence that Kelliher had been the victim of a conspiracy to obtain his money. The jury quickly returned indictments charging J.J. Webb with first degree murder and charging H.G. Neill, alias Hoodoo Brown, with larceny.

Webb was arrested Thursday afternoon, March 4, by three deputy sheriffs, but the deputies could find no trace of Hoodoo Brown. The *Optic,* on Friday, March 5, reported the arrest of Webb and added:

> *H.G. Neill, vulgarly known as "Hoo-doo Brown,"* *went east Wednesday night in company with Dutchy,* *against whom an indictment was returned by the grand* *jury.*
>
> *After the killing of Kelliher, the money in his posses-* *sion, said to be $1,950, instead of only $1,090, as given* *to the reporters, fell into the hands of Neill, who was Justice* *of the Peace and acting coroner. The funeral expenses were* *borne and Neill put the rest of the money in his pocket and* *skipped for parts unknown.*

The *Optic* said that Neill and Dutchy had boarded a train in Las Vegas on Wednesday night and had last been seen the next morning up the line at Otero, where they had had breakfast. On the way north, the newspaper said, Neill had exhibited a large roll of greenbacks to the conductor. Neill gave Dutchy $150 and the two parted, Dutchy heading to the north toward Alamosa, Colorado, and Neill heading to the east into Kansas.

In what first appeared to be an unrelated incident, the widow of Joe Carson, the town marshal who had been killed in the January 22 dance-hall battle, had the body of her late husband exhumed from a Las Vegas cemetery and boarded an eastbound train with the coffin two nights after the sudden departure of Hoodoo Brown. The *Optic* reported on Saturday, March 6:

*Mrs. Carson left for Houston, Texas, taking with her
the remains of her late husband. Mrs. Carson has had a
more varied experience than many women of her age. She
at one time served as a detective for Allen Pinkerton, but
has not been engaged in the secret service for nine months,
in deference to the wishes of her late husband.*

On Monday, March 8, the U.S. marshal's office in Parsons, Kansas, received an urgent telegram from Las Vegas, reading:

*Arrest Hyman G. Neill, alias Hoodoo Brown, about six
feet in height, light hair and mustache, weighs about 140,
slim and active, blue eyes, dressed in a plaid grey suit, going
to Houston, Texas, waiting there for a lady accompanying
the corpse of her husband. I have a warrant for him. $200
for his capture, Governor of New Mexico will undoubtedly
offer more, will take the train tomorrow for Houston.
(signed) D. Romero, Sheriff of San Miguel County, New
Mexico.*

A deputy U.S. marshal in Parsons located and arrested Neill that same day at the Belmont House, where he had been staying while awaiting the arrival of Mrs. Carson. The widow arrived on the noon train, and the *Parsons Sun* reported that "the meeting between the pair, after the man was arrested, is said to have been affecting in the extreme, and rather more affectionate than would be expected under the circumstances." Another newspaper, the *Parsons Eclipse* added that "The offense committed at Las Vegas, as near as we can gather the facts relating to it, was murder and robbery and the circumstances connected with the arrest here would indicate that the lesser crime of seduction and adultery was connected with it."

Neill, who first insisted that his name was Henry Graham, hired two local attorneys, petitioned for a writ of habeas corpus, and was released when the officers failed to show any legal authority for holding him in custody. "His female companion went south on the M.K. & T. Tuesday noon," the *Parsons Sun* reported, "he starting several hours ahead on horseback. They will doubtless meet again further south." In a proclamation signed by Acting Governor W.G. Ritch at Santa Fe on March 15, 1880, a reward of $300 was offered for the apprehension and detention of H.G. Neill and the delivery of him to the sheriff of San Miguel County.

The *Chicago Times,* reporting on the scandalous affair in Las Vegas, said that the justice of the peace, the marshal's widow, and the coffin "have been skylarking through some of the interior towns of Kansas ever since. Although Mrs. Carson still clings to her old love, she follows faithfully in the wanderings of her new mash."

The *Optic,* on March 15, published a letter it had received from Neill, mailed March 11 at Muskogee, Indian Territory, in which the fugitive said he planned to return to Las Vegas to answer the indictment against him. "I must tell you my motive for leaving Vegas as I did," he wrote, and continued:

> *I had no intention ten hours before I started. On the night that I left a man came to me and said there was going to be an indictment found against myself, Webb, and Dave Mather, for killing some one, and that I would be arrested the next day and thrown in jail. Well, this so frightened*

*me that I deliberately packed my valise and told everybody
I met that I would leave.*

Morris Kelliher, brother of the murder victim, arrived in
Las Vegas on March 10 and made arrangements to have the
remains of his brother exhumed and shipped to McHenry
County, Illinois, where their parents lived, for reburial. He
also asked to be deputized to go hunt Hoodoo Brown.

As an April Fool's joke, the *Optic* on April 1 published a
story saying that Neill had been captured, returned to Las
Vegas in chains, and was being held under guard at the St.
Nicholas Hotel in East Las Vegas. Crowds of curious persons
were taken in by the joke, flocking to the hotel to see the
prisoner. But Hyman G. Neill, alias Hoodoo Brown, had
shaken the dust of Las Vegas from his feet forever. Like Mysterious Dave, he vanished to an unknown fate.

With the sudden departure of Hoodoo Brown and Dave
Mather and the jailing of J.J. Webb for murder, the rule of the
Dodge City Gang in Las Vegas was brought to an end. There
were violent repercussions for a long time to come, however.

John Joshua Webb, sentenced to be hanged for murder, contemplates his fate in the Las Vegas jail, his legs securely shackled. (Courtesy Andy Gregg)

John Joshua Webb

John Joshua Webb was convicted of first degree murder one week after he shot and killed Michael Kelliher in the Goodlet and Roberts saloon. Testimony in the San Miguel County District Court jury trial of the thirty-four-year-old, bearded policeman was heard in the county courthouse on Tuesday, March 9, 1880. The case went to the jury at midnight, and the jury returned the first-degree murder verdict after deliberating three hours.

Although Webb testified that H.G. Neill (Hoodoo Brown) had appointed him to the East Las Vegas police force in January and that he had served until a day or two after the killing, he said he had never had a certificate of his appointment. Official books of the justice-of-the-peace office that were produced in court contained no record that Webb had ever been appointed an officer.

When the verdict was returned, an immediate defense motion for a new trial was taken under advisement by L. Bradford Prince, the presiding judge. On March 12, Judge Prince denied Webb's motion for a new trial and sentenced him to be hanged by the neck until dead on Friday, April 9.

"From an officer to a felon's cell, from a felon's cell to the gallows in thirty days is the neatness and dispatch with which judge and jury are determined business of that character shall henceforth be done in this territory," a correspondent for the *Chicago Times* wrote.

Judge Prince granted a stay of execution, however, when Webb's attorney, Sidney M. Barnes, filed notice of appeal. "Webb is a regular type of western bully, a big, burly, coarse fellow, well fitted mentally and physically for the villainous part he took in the horrible affair," the *Chicago Times* correspondent wrote. "He was rather a self appointed officer, which position he was allowed to hold partly because his reckless and fearless habits made him a very good man in quieting riotous disturbances."

Webb had had a quite varied career on the Western frontier as a teamster, miner, lumberjack, cattleman, hired gunman, and saloon keeper before arriving in Las Vegas in the fall of 1879. According to a biography of him published in the *Las Vegas Optic* at the time of his conviction, he was born in Keokuk County, Iowa, on February 13, 1847, one of eleven children of hard-working and respectable parents. The Webb family moved to Nebraska in the spring of 1862, when John Joshua was fifteen years old, and two years later, at the age of seventeen, he struck out on his own.

Denver was his first stop, and then Central City, Colorado. In the summer of 1865 he accompanied General Patrick Connor's Powder River expedition against the Sioux, apparently as a teamster. He returned to Denver the following year, and then went east into Kansas and got a job with the government beef contractor at Fort Dodge. The summer of 1867 found him in Cheyenne, Wyoming, and in the fall of that year he headed south to the new gold-mining camp of Elizabethtown, in northern New Mexico, where he spent about a year working as a miner.

In 1868 he went north to Fort Lyons, Colorado, where he hired out as a government teamster again and whacked a six-mule team to Fort Dodge, remaining there until the spring of 1869. Then his wanderings took him back to Denver, where he worked as a lumberjack in the pine forests until the fall of 1870. He then journeyed to Indian Territory to get a job at Camp Supply whacking bulls for Lee and Reynolds, the post traders.

On a trip to the North Fork of the Canadian River in 1871, he traded a small quantity of goods for some cattle, drove the cattle to Caldwell, Kansas, and bought the Old Bluff Creek Ranch near the town. Because of poor health, he sold the cattle ranch in the spring of 1872 to Curly Marshall and opened a saloon in Caldwell. Selling the Caldwell saloon in the fall of 1872, Webb returned to Fort Dodge, went south with a party of buffalo hunters, and got a job driving an ox team for A.C. Myers at Adobe Walls in the Texas Panhandle.

In 1874, he was placed in charge of a wagon train hauling supplies for General Nelson A. Miles. As an army wagonmaster in 1876, he helped move the U.S. 6th Cavalry from Fort Dodge to Santa Fe, returning to Fort Dodge with the U.S. 5th Cavalry. After more service at Camp Supply, he worked in Dodge City from the spring of 1877 to early in 1879 as a teamster for A.J. Anthony.

Webb was a member of Sheriff W.B. (Bat) Masterson's posse when it tracked down and captured several members of the Mike Rourke gang that attempted to hold up a Santa Fe Railroad depot and train at Kinsley, Kansas, east of Dodge

City, on January 27, 1878. One of the men they captured was Dave Rudabaugh, who won his freedom by agreeing to testify against his partners in crime.

Early in 1879, Webb opened the Lady Gay Saloon in Dodge City in partnership with Benjamin Springer. That summer, he was among the Dodge City gunmen hired by the Santa Fe Railroad in its fight with the Denver and Rio Grande for possession of the Royal Gorge in Colorado, the only railroad gateway to booming Leadville. While in the service of the railroad, the newspaper biography said, he "conducted himself in a praiseworthy manner, making many friends," and once refused an $8,000 bribe offered by the rival railroad. The Santa Fe Railroad gave him a $500 reward for his "faithfulness and unflinching courage."

Leaving Dodge City in the fall of 1879, Webb followed the railroad down to Las Vegas and got a job with the Adams Express Company as a special detective. Within a short time, he was considered a part of the Dodge City Gang that ruled East Las Vegas. It was this unfortunate association that brought him face to face with the gallows.

Meanwhile, Michael Kelliher was not the only visitor to Las Vegas to meet sudden death on that fateful day, March 2, 1880.

Death of a Salesman

James Morehead, a traveling salesman for several St. Louis wholesale houses, arrived in Las Vegas during the last week in February 1880 and checked in at the St. Nicholas Hotel in the new town. Morehead, a forty-year-old bachelor, was a neatly dressed man who enjoyed the finer things of life. He expected and demanded the best of service wherever he stopped, whether it was a refined Eastern city or a rough frontier town like Las Vegas.

In Las Vegas, the traveling salesman had the nerve to keep arriving in the hotel dining room late for his meals and insisting that he be served fried eggs. What happened to him as a result was brought out at the coroner's inquest a few days later. Morehead first appeared late for supper in the St. Nicholas dining room on a Friday night. He asked the waiter, twenty-three-year-old James Allen, if he could have fried eggs for his supper. The waiter, who had operated a saloon at Leadville, Colorado, before drifting on to Las Vegas, said he would ask the cook. Returning moments later, Allen told the salesman that the cook was too busy to fry any eggs, and that he would have to take his supper without them.

Saturday morning, Morehead arrived in the dining room late for breakfast and again asked for fried eggs. Allen told him that he was too late for eggs—that the cook was already preparing dinner and didn't have time to bother with them.

Morehead was late for breakfast again Sunday morning, but managed to get his eggs. Asking for eggs again that evening at supper, Morehead was told that he could have eggs after the rush was over, but when the rush had subsided, he told Allen he had lost his appetite and did not want any eggs.

Tuesday morning, March 2, Morehead once again was late for breakfast. He was in good spirits, as the day before he had sold a stock of liquor to the Charles Ilfeld Company. He asked the waiter if he could have eggs for breakfast, and Allen, losing patience, told the salesman he could always have eggs if he would just come for his meals at the proper times.

The salesman was not ready to let the matter drop, however. Words followed, and Allen told Morehead that he didn't care to hear any more about the subject. If he were dissatisfied, he should complain to the proprietor.

"You needn't get up on your left ear about it," Morehead exclaimed.

"Your constant racket about eggs is enough to put anybody on his ear," Allen retorted.

"Please go to hell," the salesman said.

"I don't care to," the waiter answered, "but you can go as quick as you want to."

Morehead stood up from the table and rolled up his sleeves.

"If you want anything out of me, you can get it," he said.

The two men went into a clinch. Morehead managed to pick Allen up and carry the struggling waiter part way across the dining room. In the scuffling, he fell over some chairs, falling to the floor with the waiter beneath him. Others in the dining room managed to separate the two men. Allen immediately ran behind the bar, picked up a beer bottle, and started for Morehead again. He dropped the bottle when he saw Morehead put his hand behind him, as if reaching for a weapon.

The waiter ran into the kitchen, borrowed a revolver from a dishwasher, and returned to the dining room door, gun in hand. He demanded that Morehead apologize. Morehead, stooping slightly, advanced slowly toward the waiter, who retreated slowly into the kitchen. When Morehead reached the kitchen door, Allen pulled the trigger. The salesman slumped to the floor, fatally wounded.

Morehead died at 10 o'clock that night, twelve hours after he was shot. A coroner's jury, after hearing the waiter's testimony, ruled that James Morehead had come to his death by a pistol shot fired by James Allen and that "the killing was willful, malicious and felonious murder, and without justification or provocation whatsoever." Allen was taken to the county jail to await trial.

Webb Declines Freedom

Two men stepped out of a hired hack in front of the San Miguel County Jail in West Las Vegas at about 2 o'clock on the afternoon of April 2, 1880, and asked the driver, Carl Caldwell, to wait for them. The two walked to the jail door and asked for admittance, saying they had come to visit the prisoner, J.J. Webb. The jailer, Antonio Lino Valdez, recognized the visitors as Dave Rudabaugh, former part-time East Las Vegas policeman, and John Llewellyn, better known as "Little Allen," a pint-sized carpenter and house painter from Georgia.

Rudabaugh had been to the jail to visit Webb on several occasions, and the jailer did not hesitate to unlock the door and permit the two to enter the jail's walled *placita,* or inner courtyard. Rudabaugh and Webb had become close friends, notwithstanding the fact that Webb had assisted in the capture of Rudabaugh after the attempted train robbery in Kansas two years before.

The two visitors walked across the *placita* to Webb's cell, and Rudabaugh handed the prisoner a newspaper. At that moment, Little Allen asked Valdez to hand him the keys to

Webb's cell. When Valdez replied that he could not and would not, Allen drew his revolver and shot the jailer in the chest. The two took the cell keys from the fallen jailer, threw them into Webb's cell, and ran back across the *placita* and out the door, shouting to Webb to free himself.

Jumping into the waiting hack, the two ordered the driver at gunpoint to drive them quickly to East Las Vegas. The driver whipped the horses down the street and across the Gallinas River bridge. Reaching the new town, the two passengers kicked the driver out into the street, and Rudabaugh took the reins. They paused briefly at Houghton's Hardware Store, grabbed a number of carbines and rifles, threw the weapons into the hack, climbed in, and whipped the horses into a run east out of town.

A small, four-man posse that had been hastily organized followed the departing hack on horseback, pursuing it across the meadows east of the community. The pursuers came close enough to exchange shots with the fugitives, several of their bullets smashing into the back of the hack, but they exhausted their ammunition and retired back to town.

A larger posse, which took to the trail later, found the hack abandoned by the side of the road. At a sheep camp about twenty-five miles from town they found the hack horses, which were owned by J.M. Talbot of Las Vegas. Sheepherders in the camp said that two men had forced them to give them some good saddle horses for the hack horses. The posse returned to town without Rudabaugh and Allen, who had vanished into the plains.

Back at the jail, Webb was still secure in his cell, however, having passed up the opportunity to unlock his cell and escape. Valdez, the jailer, had been carried into the jail kitchen, where he died of the bullet wound he had sustained in his chest.

Less than a week later, on April 8, the county jail received another prisoner, George Davidson, charged with murder in the fatal shooting early that morning of twenty-two-year-old Nelson W. (Nick) Starbird, a Las Vegas hack driver. The shooting had occurred at about 3 o'clock that morning on the Hot Springs Road in West Las Vegas, to the rear of the Catholic Church, as Starbird was driving two passengers to their homes from East Las Vegas. The passengers were George Poindexter, a monte dealer, who was believed to be carrying a large sum of money, and a Mexican musician known as Vitorio.

Starbird saw three men standing to one side of the road just ahead of him, and fearing trouble, attempted to drive quickly by them. One of the men cried "Hold on," firing at the hack at the same moment. Starbird threw his hands up and exclaimed, "Oh, my God, I'm shot in the arm; take the reins, I'm fainting." Poindexter grabbed the reins and drove the hack on up the road a short distance. The assailants disappeared down the road in the darkness. Starbird, bleeding profusely, rolled over and died in the hack, having been shot in the left shoulder. A native of New York, he had arrived in Las Vegas the year before from Hutchison, Kansas.

The *Las Vegas Optic* said it was believed the bullet was meant for Poindexter, the gambler, in a robbery attempt. Four Lincoln County teamsters were arrested hours later in connection with the fatal shooting, but all but Davidson were released for lack of evidence.

That same day—April 8, 1880—a notice was published in the *Las Vegas Optic* warning murderers, confidence men, and thieves "that they must either leave this town or conform themselves to the requirements of law, or they will be summarily dealt with." The notice, signed "Vigilantes," appears in full at the beginning of this book.

By this time East Las Vegas had a population of 1,500, about the same as West Las Vegas on the opposite bank of the stream, and increasing numbers of law-abiding citizens had become determined to put a stop to the steady stream of violence that had made the community notorious on the Western frontier. The published threat of Vigilante justice apparently cleared Las Vegas of much of its rabble, particularly when word got around that the "committee of one hundred" was backing up its warning with a squad of riflemen who would conceal themselves around town and shoot on sight any of the better-known desperadoes who might happen by. The violence subsided for the first time since the arrival of the railroad the summer before, with only a few sporadic incidents in the months that followed.

Webb Tastes Freedom

It was discovered on Wednesday morning, November 10, 1880, that six prisoners had escaped from the San Miguel County Jail in West Las Vegas. The escapees apparently had picked the lock of their cell door during the night and had walked out the unlocked front door of the jail without waking any of the guards. Las Vegas newspapers speculated that the guards, perhaps, had been bribed. The escaped prisoners included:

> *J.J. Webb, whose appeal of his murder conviction in the shooting of Micahel Kelliher was still pending in the New Mexico Territorial Supreme Court.*
>
> *George Davidson, the Lincoln County teamster, still awaiting trial on a charge of murdering Nelson (Nick) Starbird, the Las Vegas hack driver.*
>
> *James Allen, the hotel waiter, who in August had been convicted of first-degree murder in the death of James Morehead, the traveling salesman.*
>
> *John Murray, indicted on a charge of murdering a Tecolote gardner.*

George Davis, indicted on a charge of stealing mules.
William Mullen, indicted for complicity in the Las
Vegas train robbery a year before.

San Miguel County Sheriff Desiderio Romero led a posse
in pursuit of the escaped prisoners. On Thursday evening,
November 11, they came upon the six fugitives camped near
Chaperito on the Gallinas River southeast of Las Vegas. The
posse charged into the camp to open a brief but hot gun battle.
Moments later, James Allen and George Davidson were dead
on the ground and their companions had scattered. The posse
continued the chase, rounding up Mullen and Murray. Only
Webb and Davis remained at large. Some said Las Vegas
lawmen had secretly arranged the jailbreak so that the escaping prisoners could be killed.

Meanwhile, Patrick F. Garrett, newly elected sheriff of
Lincoln County to the south, was leading a large posse in the
lower Pecos River Valley in search of Henry McCarty, alias
William H. Bonney, alias Billy the Kid, and members of his
gang of livestock rustlers. At daybreak on November 26,
Garrett and his posse surrounded the Dedrick ranch house at
Bosque Grande on the Pecos River, hoping to find the Kid
inside. Instead of the Kid and his companions, the trap yielded
Webb and Davis.

The posse took their two prisoners north to Fort Sumner,
arriving there early the next morning. Garrett sent word to
Sheriff Romero at Las Vegas that Webb and Davis had been
captured, and asked the sheriff to come after them. Leaving
four members of his posse at Fort Sumner to guard the prisoners, Garrett took the rest of his men and resumed the hunt for
Billy the Kid. Returning to Fort Sumner a few days later,

Garrett found that Webb and Davis were still under guard there, and that nothing had been heard from the San Miguel County sheriff.

Garrett decided to take the prisoners to Las Vegas himself to get them off his hands. He dismissed all his possemen except Barney Mason, and hired C.B. Hoadley to convey the prisoners north to Las Vegas in a wagon, with himself and Mason as guards. Meanwhile, Deputy Sheriff Francisco Romero and a four-man posse had arrived in Puerto de Luna from Las Vegas, on their way south to take charge of the two prisoners. They picked up from twenty to twenty-five more men at Puerto de Luna and continued south toward Fort Sumner. Garrett and Mason, with their two prisoners and the wagon driver, met the large posse on the road about eight miles south of Puerto de Luna. Writing of the meeting in his book, *The Authentic Life of Billy the Kid,* Garrett said:

> *They were all mounted, and came down upon my little party like a whirlwind of lunatics—their steeds prancing and curveting—with loud boasts and swaggering airs— one would have thought they had taken a contract to fight the (Civil War) battle of Valverde over again, and that an army of ten thousand rebels opposed them instead of two manacled prisoners.*

All proceeded to Puerto de Luna, where the two prisoners were placed in irons. Webb, who expressed fears of the mob that was to take him and Davis on to Las Vegas, offered Garrett all the money he had—ten dollars—if he would accompany them. Garrett declined the cash offer, but agreed to go on to Las Vegas with them.

Patrick F. "Pat" Garrett, New Mexico lawman who protected his prisoners, Billy the Kid and Dave Rudabaugh, from a Las Vegas mob. (Courtesy Museum of New Mexico, negative 46217)

Garrett later wrote that he was completely disgusted with the boisterous conduct of the possemen. He commented in his book, published in 1882, that Dave Rudabaugh had once remarked "it only required lightning bugs and corn cobs to stampede officers of Las Vegas or Puerto de Luna."

Garrett accompanied the posse and the prisoners to within a few miles of Las Vegas, where they stopped at a wayside inn to have some drinks. "I seized the opportunity to escape their objectionable society, and rode on, alone, into town," Garrett wrote. "I was ashamed to be seen with the noisy, gabbling, boasting, senseless, undignified mob, whose deportment would have disgusted the Kid and his band of thieves." One can only wonder if these were Garrett's actual words, or those of his friend and ghost writer, Marshall Ashmun (Ash) Upson, itinerant New Mexico journalist who had edited a newspaper in Las Vegas in the early 1870s.

Webb and Davis, meanwhile, were once again confined in the San Miguel County Jail.

Capture of Rudabaugh

Dave Rudabaugh, following his flight from Las Vegas in a stolen hack after his attempt to free J.J. Webb from jail, was soon reported to be a member of Billy the Kid's gang of rustlers in the lower Pecos River Valley of New Mexico. Mystery, however, surrounded the fate of his companion, John Llewellyn, better known as "Little Allen," who had shot and killed the jailer, Antonio Lino Valdez.

Years later, on December 4, 1896, the *Las Vegas Optic* published an article giving an account of what had happened to Allen under a headline reading "A Little Bit of History." The newspaper quoted an article that had appeared in *Field and Stream,* written by a man who said he had obtained the story from Rudabaugh himself. Allen, according to this story, suffered from both tuberculosis and rheumatism. The long hours in the saddle as he rode south with Rudabaugh from Las Vegas proved too much for him, and unable to obtain medical attention, he kept pleading with Rudabaugh to shoot him and put him out of his misery. As the two were riding along one day on the open range, Rudabaugh suddenly pulled his pistol, placed it close to his companion's head, and pulled the trigger.

He buried Allen in some sand along the road near Alkali Wells, the article said.

Rudabaugh achieved the reputation of being Billy the Kid's right-hand man during the months that followed. In Las Vegas, however, he was remembered principally for his part in the fatal shooting of the popular jailer.

Rudabaugh's career on the Western frontier is almost as shadowy as that of Dave Mather. R.A. Cameron, a U.S. postal inspector who had investigated him for mail robbery, wrote in 1882 that Rudabaugh had started his desperate career in Ohio in about 1870 when at the age of seventeen he held up and robbed an express car on a train near his home. He made a big haul in this robbery, Cameron said, and apparently fled to Arkansas.

Cameron's impressions of Rudabaugh were published in the *Denver Tribune* early in 1882 and reprinted in the *Optic* on March 3 of that year. His description of Rudabaugh, as published in the newspapers, said that:

> *He is thick set and athletic in build; is about five-feet nine-inches in height. He is suave and very gentlemanly in his deportment. He has brown hair, hazel eyes and a heavy mustache of a shade of brown lighter than that of his hair.*
>
> *He is fluent in speech, mildly argumentive in disposition, and has that peculiar faculty of being able to obtain news and facts where others would fail. This is a faculty which he uses advantageously in his search for express news on railroads.*
>
> *He is as brave as a lion and a natural born organizer. He gathers a gang and has it in working condition within a few days. He is always clear-headed, has the cunning of*

a fox, and never falls into a position of unnecessary danger through the recklessness of bravery or dissipation.

According to other reports at the time, Rudabaugh and Dave Mather had been members of a gang of rustlers in Arkansas in the early 1870s along with Milton J. Yarberry, who was hanged in Albuquerque in 1883 after being convicted of murder while serving as town constable. When arrested in Kansas in 1878 for attempted train robbery, Rudabaugh was described by a Dodge City newspaper as "a good-looking specimen of the border ruffian." His association with Billy the Kid's gang lasted about nine months.

On December 26, 1880, sheriff-elect Pat Garrett of Lincoln County, who a month before had delivered the escaped prisoner Webb back to Las Vegas, brought Rudabaugh back to town, along with Billy the Kid and two other members of the gang, Tom Pickett and Billy Wilson. The tall and lanky Garrett, who had been elected sheriff of Lincoln County on November 8 but had not yet officially assumed the office, had taken custody of the four in his role as a deputy U.S. marshal.

Las Vegas, according to the local newspapers, was thrown into a fever of excitement by the news of the capture and delivery of the outlaws. The *Las Vegas Gazette,* on December 27, reported that:

> *The greatest excitement prevailed yesterday afternoon when the news was noised abroad that Pat Garrett and Frank Stewart had arrived in town bringing with them Billy "the Kid," the notorious outlaw and three of his gang. People stood on the muddy street corners and in hotel*

offices and saloons talking of the great event. The excitement
and interest can scarcely be imagined. . . .

A little after 4 o'clock yesterday afternoon a two-mule
wagon hauling four or five men besides the driver, with
three men on horseback came at a good gait up the old Santa
Fe trail. They kept on past the plaza and drew up at the
jail. The few who were on the streets followed the little
cavalcade, but their curiosity was only slightly satisfied, for
without any ceremony the crowd was quickly within the
jail.

The announcement was made that the party com-
prised Billy "the Kid," captain of the gang that has been
making its headquarters at Las Portales; Dave Ruda-
baugh, his desperate lieutenant who killed López (Valdez)
the jailer in this city the first of last April; Billy Wilson,
the slick young fellow who has been passing counterfeit
money, and Tom Pickett, the ex-policeman of Vegas who
was reported to have been killed in Sumner one week ago.
News of their arrival ran like wildfire about town and
everyone was on the que vive for particulars of the
capture. . . .

Details of the capture were published by both Las Vegas newspapers.

The *Optic* recalled that Frank Stewart, a detective employed by the Canadian River Cattlemen's Association in the
Texas Panhandle, had left Las Vegas on December 14 with a
group of Texas cowboys bound south for Fort Sumner. Their
object was to join forces with Garrett and his New Mexico
posse, track down the Kid and his gang, and recover cattle
they had been rustling in Texas.

The combined posses were at Fort Sumner on the night of December 19 when the Kid and five companions, riding in pairs through a light falling snow, entered the quiet community and the trap that had been set for them. Garrett and his men opened fire, and Tom O'Folliard, who was riding at the head of the outlaw group with Pickett, fell from his horse, mortally wounded. The others turned their horses quickly and disappeared in the snow and fog. Rudabaugh, whose horse had been shot, rode it until it dropped dead, then doubled up with one of his companions.

As the snowstorm grew in intensity, Garrett and his men weathered the storm at Fort Sumner before taking to the trail of the outlaws. When the storm subsided, they rode out of town and headed east across the snow-covered plain. After traveling about a dozen miles, they picked up the trail of the outlaws at a ranch, and followed the trail through the snow another three miles to Stinking Springs, an old sheep camp, where the Kid and his followers were holed up in a small, primitive rock house.

The possemen, arriving at the spot before sunrise on December 24, took up positions outside the rock shelter, and waited for the dawn. Came the dawn, and a figure appeared in the doorway of the house. Garrett and his men, thinking it was the Kid, opened fire. The figure staggered, braced himself for a moment against the door post, stepped back inside, then reeled back outside toward the concealed lawmen. They heard him say, "I wish . . . ," before falling dead in the snow without finishing the sentence. It was not the Kid, but his close friend and companion, Charlie Bowdre.

The siege, thus started, lasted until late in the afternoon, when the Kid and his three surviving companions, Rudabaugh, Pickett, and Wilson, surrendered and handed over their weapons. The prisoners were transported north to Las Vegas in a borrowed wagon, captors and prisoners pausing at Puerto de Luna for Christmas dinner at the home of Polish immigrant Alexander Grzelachowski, a Roman Catholic priest turned merchant and rancher.

The *Gazette* identified the posse members who had arrived in Las Vegas with the prisoners: "Besides Garrett and Frank Stewart, in the party who brought the gang into Vegas, there were J.N. East and F.W. Emory of the (Texas) Panhandle and Barney Mason."

Reporters for both the *Gazette* and the *Optic* interviewed the prisoners in the jail the morning after they were brought in. The *Optic* gave a brief sketch of each prisoner:

THE PRISONERS

Kid is about 24 years of age, and has a bold yet pleasant countenance. When interviewed between the bars at the jail this morning, he was in a talkative mood, but said that anything he might say would not be believed by the people.

He laughed heartily when informed that the papers of the Territory had built him up a reputation second only to that of (Apache chief) Victorio. Kid claims never to have had a large number of men with him, and that the few who were with him when captured were employed on a ranch. This is his statement and is given for what it is worth.

DAVE RUDABAUGH

looks and dresses about the same as when in Las Vegas, apparently not having made any raids upon clothing stores. His face is weather-beaten from long exposure. This is the only noticeable difference. Radabaugh [sic] inquired some-

what anxiously in regard to the feeling in the community and was told that it was very strong against him. He remarked that the papers had all published exaggerated reports of the depredations of Kid's party in the lower country. It was not half so bad as has been reported.

TOM PICKETT

Tom, who was once a policeman in West Las Vegas, greeted everybody with a hearty grip of the hand and seemed reasonably anxious to undergo an examination. Pickett is well connected, but has led a wild career. His father lives in Decatur, Wise county, Texas, and has served as a member of the Legislature. All the home property was once mortgaged to keep Pickett out of prison, but he unfeelingly skipped the country, betraying the confidence of his own mother.

BILLY WILSON,

the other occupant of the cell, reclined leisurely on some blankets in the corner of the apartment and his meditations were not disturbed by our Faber pusher.

The *Gazette* reporter wrote that he arrived at the jail as Mike Cosgrove, a mail contractor, was delivering a good suit of clothes to each of the four prisoners, saying that he wanted "to see the boys go away in style," knowing that they soon would be transported to a Santa Fe jail. The *Gazette* said the Kid looked and acted a mere boy, adding:

He is about five feet eight or nine inches tall, slightly built and lithe, weighing about 140; a frank open countenance, looking like a school boy, with the traditional silky fuzz on his upper lip; clear blue eyes, with a rougish snap about them; light hair and complexion. He is, in all, quite a handsome looking fellow, the only imperfection being two prominent front teeth slightly protruding like squirrel's teeth, and he has agreeable and winning ways.

"You appear to take it easy," the *Gazette* reporter said.

"Yes. What's the use of looking on the gloomy side of everything," the Kid answered. "The laugh's on me this time."

Then, looking around the walled jail yard, the Kid asked, "Is the jail in Santa Fe any better than this? This is a terrible place to put a fellow in."

That afternoon, December 27, the Kid, Rudabaugh, and Wilson were taken from the jail by Garrett, Stewart, and others and escorted to the railroad depot, where they were placed aboard a westbound passenger train for conveyance to Santa Fe. An angry crowd gathered at the depot, demanding that Rudabaugh be left behind. The *Optic* reported the disturbance:

> *As the train was ready to leave the depot, an unsuccessful attempt was made by Sheriff Romero to secure Radabaugh [sic] and return him to the county jail. The engineer of the outgoing train was covered by guns, and ordered not to move his engine. If the sheriff had been as plucky as some of the citizens who urged him forward, the matter would have been settled without any excitement whatever. The prisoner, Radabaugh, the only one wanted, was virtually in the hands of the United States authorities, having been arrested by deputy United States marshals, and they were in duty bound to deliver him to the authorities in Santa Fe.*

Billy the Kid, who thought the Las Vegas jail was "a terrible place to put a fellow in." (Courtesy Museum of New Mexico, negative 30769)

The sheriff and a few picked, trusty men might have gone over to Santa Fe with the party, and, after Radabaugh's delivery, brought him back to Las Vegas, where he is badly wanted, not only by the Mexicans, but by all Americans who desire to see the law vindicated.

The excitement at the depot delayed the departure of the train for about forty-five minutes, but Garrett held on to his prisoners, threatening to arm them if that proved necessary for their own protection. Billy the Kid seemed to enjoy the commotion, pointing a make-believe gun out a car window at some children standing alongside the tracks and saying "Bang, bang, bang."

"As the train rolled out," the *Gazette* said, "he (the Kid) lifted his hat and invited us to call and see him in Santa Fe, calling out adios."

In spite of his happy-go-lucky attitude, the Kid was being hauled off to face murder charges that had been brought in connection with several killings during the Lincoln County War in southeastern New Mexico in 1878. He assumed that Gov. Lew Wallace would take time out from his gubernatorial duties and his writing of the novel *Ben Hur* in Santa Fe to extend to him the amnesty he had offered to all participants in the civil conflict during his efforts to end the warfare. But the young outlaw's letters to the New Mexico governor, written from the Santa Fe jail a few blocks away, went unanswered.

Rudabaugh's Confession

Most of those accused of the two stagecoach robberies and the train robbery near Las Vegas in 1879 had been languishing in jail for more than a year when Dave Rudabaugh was brought in. Only one had been cleared of the charge against him. That was William Clancy, alias John Clark, the railroad worker, who on August 2, 1880, had been found not guilty by a U.S. District Court jury in Santa Fe of an indictment charging him with mail robbery in connection with the stagecoach holdup of August 18, 1879. The same charge was still pending against his co-defendant, Antonio López, the Chilean.

Still in jail in Santa Fe were the four who had been indicted for mail robbery in connection with the second stagecoach holdup of August 30, 1879. They were Jordan L. Webb, Frank Cady, John Pierce, alias Bull Shit Jack, and William Nicholson, alias Slap Jack Bill, the Pride of the Panhandle. Jordan Webb had been brought to trial twice in 1880, on February 28 and on August 7, the jury failing to agree on a verdict each time. Still in jail in Las Vegas were the Stokes brothers, Joseph and William, charged with the train robbery.

Their co-defendant, William Mullen, "the Pock-Marked Kid," had been released.

Jordan Webb went on trial for the third time in the U.S. District Court in Santa Fe on February 11, 1881, and this time his defense attorneys introduced a surprise witness, Dave Rudabaugh, who had been escorted to the courtroom from his cell in the Santa Fe jail. Rudabaugh's testimony at Webb's trial was summed up the next day in Santa Fe's *Daily New Mexican:*

> *Rudabaugh stated that he was at the head of the gang which robbed the stage on both occasions; that at the time of the first robbery he had two companions and at the time of the second three; and that the defendant, Webb, was present on neither occasion. No amount of persuasion or threats would induce him to give the names of those who were connected with him in the robbery. . . .*

Jordan Webb was promptly acquitted, and all those who had been held in connection with the stagecoach robberies were released from custody. Reported the *Las Vegas Optic* on February 14:

> *All parties arrested for complicity in the robbery of a stage coach some months ago have been acquitted and released. . . . There remains no doubt that they were the victims of a conspiracy and have been suffering for crimes committed by others, some of whom are now in the clutches of the law, and it is hoped that all the others soon will be. Dave Radebaugh [sic] boldly testified that he led the attack on the stage, and was quite certain that Jordan Webb,*

one of the accused on trial, was not present. He refused
to divulge the names of the robbers, whom he claims to
know. . . .

Rudabaugh never identified his accomplices, but speculation has produced such prime candidates as Mysterious Dave Mather and Joe Carson, members of Hoodoo Brown's police force, as well as Doc Holliday. It was generally believed that the justice of the peace and his officers conspired to engineer the robberies and place the blame on innocent victims.

Federal indictments were returned against Rudabaugh in Santa Fe on February 14 charging him with robbing the mails in connection with the two stagecoach robberies and with attempted mail robbery in connection with the train holdup. He pleaded guilty to all three indictments the following day, his confession of the train robbery resulting in freedom for the Stokes brothers.

The presiding judge, L. Bradford Prince, gave Rudabaugh a suspended life sentence on February 26, and ordered U.S. Marshal John Sherman to turn the prisoner over to the sheriff of San Miguel County to stand trial on the more serious charge of first-degree murder in connection with the fatal shooting of Antonio Lino Valdez, the Las Vegas jailer. A San Miguel County grand jury had indicted him on this charge in August 1880.

Rudabaugh, who had provided freedom for others by his confessions, now decided to provide some freedom for himself. His attempt to break out of the Santa Fe jail, along with his pals Billy the Kid and Billy Wilson, was described in the Santa Fe *New Mexican* and copied by the *Las Vegas Gazette* on March 2, 1881, a day or so later:

*Yesterday afternoon it was discovered that the Kid
and his gang had concocted and were stealthily carrying out
a plan by which they hoped to gain their freedom and escape
the fate that awaits them. And very fortunate it was that
the discovery was made just when it was, for a night or two
more would have sufficed for completion of the well laid
scheme. It appears that Sheriff Romulo Martinez fearing
that the four desperate men, the Kid, Rudabaugh, Billy
Wilson and (Edward M.) Kelly, would ere long make a
desperate effort to get out, had promised to pay one of the
prisoners if he would assist the guard in keeping watch, and
yesterday the fellow informed him that the men were trying
to dig out. Sheriff Martinez, accompanied by Deputy Marshal (Tony) Neis, at once proceeded to the jail, and entering
the cell, found the men at supper. They examined the room
and found that the bed ticking was filled with stones and
earth, and removing the mattress discovered a deep hole.
Further investigation showed that the men had dug themselves nearly out, and by concealing the loose earth in the
bed and covering the hole up with it had almost reached the
street without awakening the suspicion of the guard. Last
night they were closely guarded and heavily ironed, and
today further precautions will be taken.*

Rudabaugh, fearing a lynch mob in Las Vegas, asked the
court that his murder trial be held in Santa Fe. His request was
granted. A Santa Fe jury convicted him of the murder charge
on April 22, and Judge Prince ordered that he be taken to Las
Vegas and hanged by the neck on May 20, 1881. Judge Prince
granted a stay of execution, however, pending an appeal of the
conviction. Rudabaugh was taken back to Las Vegas and

placed in the San Miguel County jail to await the outcome of his appeal.

Edward M. Kelly, who had attempted to dig out of the Santa Fe jail with Rudabaugh and the Kid, was being held there at the time on a charge of murdering John Reardon, a miner, at the mining camp of Carbonateville, a short distance south of Santa Fe. Kelly, a Louisiana native, was a member of a railroad construction crew in the Las Vegas area in the winter of 1879–1880 when Joe Carson, the town marshal, grub-staked him to go prospecting in the Cerrillos district south of Santa Fe. Kelly used the money to buy a partnership with James M. Thompson in a Carbonateville dance hall.

During a heated argument with Reardon on October 13, 1880, Kelly had picked up a rifle and shot him in the hip, inflicting a fatal wound. A jury in Las Vegas convicted him of first-degree murder in March 1881, shortly after his attempt to escape from jail, and he was sentenced to be hanged. Appeals were taken, and in an unusual move, President Chester A. Arthur commuted Kelly's death sentence to life imprisonment on June 10, 1882.

Billy the Kid, meanwhile, was removed from the Santa Fe jail on April 4, 1881, one month after the escape attempt, and was transported by train south to Mesilla to face murder charges in connection with his role in the Lincoln County War of 1878. He was convicted of murder for his part in the ambush slaying of Lincoln County Sheriff William Brady, and Judge Warren Bristol ordered that he be taken to the town of Lincoln, scene of the crime, there to be hanged until dead on May 13.

On April 28, while awaiting execution in Lincoln, the Kid escaped from custody after shooting to death his two guards,

J.W. Bell and Bob Olinger. Sheriff Pat Garrett, accompanied by two deputies, later followed his trail east to Fort Sumner, and there Garrett shot and killed the young outlaw on the night of July 14.

The *Santa Fe Weekly Democrat,* on July 21, 1881, published the story of Billy the Kid's death in a sardonic vein under the headline "Obituary—With His Boots Off." According to the article:

> *Billy Bonny, alias Antrim, alias Billy the Kid, the 21-year-old desperado, who is known to have killed 16 men, and who boasted that he had killed a man for every year of his life, will no more take deliberate aim at his fellow man and kill him, just to keep himself in practice. He is dead; and he died so suddenly that he did not have time to be interviewed by a preacher, or to sing hymns, or pray, before that vital spark had flown, so we cannot say positively that he had clum the shining ladder and entered the pearly gates.*
>
> *The bullet that struck him left a pistol in the hands of Pat Garrett, at Ft. Sumner, last Saturday morning about half past 12 a.m., in the room of Pete Maxwell. Gov. (Lew) Wallace will now breathe easier, as well as many others he threatened to shoot on sight.*
>
> *No sooner had the floor caught his descending form, which had a pistol in one hand and a knife in the other, than there was a strong odor of brimstone in the air, and a dark figure, with the wings of a dragon, claws like a tiger, eyes like balls of fire and horns like a bison, hovered over the corpse for a moment, and with a fiendish laugh*

*said "Ha, ha, this is my meat" and then sailed off through
a window. He did not leave his card, but he is a gentleman
well known to us by reputation, and thereby hangs a
"tail."*

The Optic, on July 25, published this item:

*An esteemed friend of the Optic at Fort Sumner, L. W.
Hale, has sent us the index finger of "Billy, the Kid," the
one which has snapped many a man's life into eternity. It
is well-preserved in alcohol and has been viewed by many
in our office today. If the rush continues we shall purchase
a small tent and open a side show to which complimentary
tickets will be issued to our personal friends.*

Later, on September 10, the *Optic* reported that the Kid's
body, minus the trigger finger, had been brought to Las Vegas
by "a fearless skelologist of this county." The article said he
had proceeded to the Fort Sumner cemetery, and in the darkness of night, with the help of a companion, had dug up the
remains five days after their burial and carried them off in a
wagon. The body was delivered to a Las Vegas "sawbones,"
the article claimed, who planned to clean the skeleton, wire
it together, and then shellac it and make it presentable for
display.

Nine days later, the *Optic* reported that it had just received a letter from a young lady, Kate Tenney of Oakland,
California, asking that she be sent the Kid's finger, along with
a picture of him. The *Optic* said it responded that it had just
sold the finger for $150 cash, and that the Kid would never

sit still long enough to have his picture taken. But it should be remembered that the newspaper editor, Russ Kistler, was quite a practical joker, a prime example being his "April Fool" story the year before about Hoodoo Brown being captured and returned to town.

Bye Bye, Birds

L̶as Vegas maintained its reputation in 1881 as the toughest town on the Western frontier.

In an apparent call for renewed Vigilante justice, the *Las Vegas Optic* editorialized on July 25:

> *The lawless conduct on our streets at night is hortful (hateful?) and disgraceful in the extreme and should not be tolerated a moment longer. The remedy is a good police force, and, in the meantime, a committee of citizens should take the matter in hand. This paragraph is worthy of thought.*

The editorial followed a newspaper report two days before that William Morgan, chief of police in West Las Vegas, had killed Victor Trujillo "and another Mexican" after going to a dance hall to quell a disturbance.

The periodic sounds of gunfire and other commotions in the streets probably reached the ears of Dave Rudabaugh and J.J. Webb, confined in the county jail pending appeals of their convictions. Rudabaugh still faced the gallows, but Webb's

189

death sentence had been commuted to life imprisonment in March by New Mexico Gov. Lew Wallace. Rudabaugh and Webb were confined in the middle cell of the jail with three other prisoners, Thomas Duffy, held for the murder of Thomas Bishop, a store clerk at the town of Liberty; H.S. Wilson; and A. Murphy, held for burglary and robbery.

In September, somebody managed to smuggle a gun to Rudabaugh. At about 3 o'clock on the morning of September 19, 1881, the prisoners picked the lock of their cell with a piece of bent wire and crept silently into the hallway leading to the jail *placita,* or courtyard. Asleep in the hallway were the three jail guards, Florenzo Mares, Guadalupe Hidalgo, and Herculano Chávez.

Rudabaugh, for some reason, paused over the figure of the sleeping Mares and awakened him by calling him by name, "Florenzo . . . Florenzo." Mares awoke to find Rudabaugh standing over him with a revolver in his hand. Without a word, Mares sprang to his feet and began grappling with the prisoner. Rudabaugh fired a shot at Mares, which missed its mark but awakened the other two guards. They rushed to Mares' assistance.

A desperate, hand-to-hand struggle between the guards and the prisoners moved into the *placita.* Rudabaugh got off one more shot before he was overpowered. Duffy, who had come to his assistance, was knocked to the floor. Before he could get up he was shot in the head by the guard, Chávez.

Wilson and Murphy, meanwhile, were attempting to scale the stone wall around the courtyard, but were caught and returned to their cell, along with Rudabaugh. Duffy died about twelve hours after he was shot. Webb, for the second time, had passed up a Rudabaugh-engineered opportunity to escape and had taken no part in the melee. A search of the prisoners' cell yielded a piece of wire, a file, and a chisel.

Webb did not pass up a third opportunity to escape. At breakfast in the jail on Saturday morning, December 3, 1881, it was discovered that seven prisoners had escaped during the night through a small hole, measuring nineteen by seven inches, that had been hacked through the stone wall of one of the cells.

The *Optic,* reporting the mass escape that evening, identified the escaped prisoners as Dave Rudabaugh, J.J. Webb, T. Quilian, who had been arrested in Santa Fe by Pat Garrett on a charge of killing a deputy sheriff in Clay County, Texas, and four men identified only as Schroder, Kelly, Goodman, and Kearney, who had been jailed for minor offenses. Officers learned the details of the escape from four prisoners who had remained behind, identified as Griffin, Rogers, Fogerty the Cuter, and Jack McManus. They said the escaped prisoners, using a knife and a handless pick, had spent much of the night digging and cutting through the cement and heavy stones of the wall, dropping the debris silently into soft mattresses. Goodman, the smallest of the group, had squeezed through the small hole and was the first one out. The other six had to remove their clothing before squeezing through. Once outside, the *Optic* reported, they put on their clothes and took to their heels.

Rudabaugh had cut the chains of his wristlets and leg shackles, allowing him freedom of movement, but the iron bands remained on his wrists and ankles. It was reported that Rudabaugh, Webb, and Quilian had paused briefly at the St. Nicholas Hotel for a short conference with Quilian's wife before leaving town.

Early that morning, a man who lived near the railroad tracks about two miles south of Las Vegas, noticed two men walking together down the tracks in the gray light of dawn. Dangling from the legs of one of the men were chains, the ends of which bounced along the ground. The two undoubtedly were Rudabaugh and Webb, leaving Las Vegas as they had come, with the railroad.

The *Optic*, which told the story of the escape under a headline reading "Bye Bye, Birds," predicted that Rudabaugh and Webb, the last remaining figures of the Dodge City Gang, had made good their escape and would never be seen in Las Vegas again. The prophesy proved to be an accurate one. Webb and Rudabaugh soon parted company, Webb heading for Arkansas, Rudabaugh for the Mexican border. In April 1882, Las Vegas received news that Webb had died of smallpox in Arkansas, four months after his escape.

Details of his death were told that month in a letter received by the mayor of Dodge City, Kansas, and published in the Dodge City *Times:*

> *Dear Sir: John J. Webb is dead. He died on the 12th inst. of smallpox in Winslow, Arkansas. He was there working for J.D. Scott & Co., on the St. L. & S.F. RR. He had the best attention and care, but there came a sudden change in the weather and I suppose he caught cold, and he died very suddenly. He was going under the name of Sam King, after he came here. You can tell the friends of his death. (signed) J.A. Scott.*

Rudabaugh, meanwhile, was reported to be seen periodically during several years after his escape in various towns along the Mexican border, in southern Arizona and Chihuahua.

His fate was told by the *Albuquerque Evening Democrat* in a brief article published on January 16, 1886: "Dave Rudebaugh, a former wicked and lawless character of Las Vegas, was killed at Parral, Mexico, a short time ago. He killed two men in the fracas that settled his own hash." Later reports said that a large group of Parral citizens had ambushed and slain Rudabaugh one night on a dark street of the Mexican town minutes after he had shot and killed two Parral residents in a *cantina* where he had been drunk and boisterous. The citizens then cut off his head, placed it on a pole, and paraded it around the streets in a torchlight procession.

Navajo Frank

The following item appeared in the *Santa Fe Daily Democrat* on Tuesday, June 27, 1882:

> *Navajo Frank has funny ideas regarding amusement. As he rode through Las Vegas upon Saturday evening, he saw old Mr. Hunter and wife quietly wending their way homeward. Funny Navajo Frank gracefully dropped his lariat over the old gentlemen's shoulders, and starting his horse at a rapid pace dragged his victim over sharp stones and rough ground. He wound up his fun by cutting the lariat and leaving the victim horribly mutilated.*
>
> *The Las Vegas folks also have funny ideas regarding amusement. They heard of Navajo Frank's fun and they hunted for him and sent him to the other side of the Eu-ropean plan. Now he has wings.*

The *Las Vegas Daily Optic* reprinted the Democrat story a few days later with the comment that the Santa Fe newspaper had a rather funny way of reporting tragedies. Mr. Hunter, the old gentleman, survived the ordeal—but Navajo Frank did not survive his.

Navajo Frank, it was said, was a full-blooded Navajo Indian who was born on the Bosque Redondo Indian Reservation at Fort Sumner in the 1860s while his people were being held captive there. As a child he was sold for five dollars to Julian Mares, a Taos sheep rancher, although it was not said who the seller was. Mares put the Indian boy to work herding sheep by the time he was seven years old, and apparently gave him the Hispanic name, Francisco Tafoya.

Navajo Frank, as he became known, developed into an expert sheepherder, going eventually into business for himself. One day he took 500 head of his employer's sheep and started south with them for the Pecos River country. Mares intercepted him a short distance below Las Vegas and relieved him of the sheep, but allowed him to continue on.

Navajo Frank, minus the sheep, found his way to Lucien B. Maxwell's home at Fort Sumner, site of the former Bosque Redondo Reservation where he had been born. Maxwell put him to work as a cowpuncher, and he remained there until he got acquainted with some Colorado freighters and decided to take up bullwhacking as a career.

He apparently was working as a freighter in 1877 when he made a brief but unforgettable appearance at El Moro, Colorado, a few miles northeast of Trinidad. The Indian walked into George Close's crowded dance hall in El Moro one night that year and offered to trade his rifle for a bottle of whiskey. Close turned him down, it being illegal to sell whiskey to Indians. Navajo Frank stalked out the door, walked over to some railroad tracks, and sat down on a railroad tie facing the dance hall.

The sounds of music, dancing, and laughter issued from the brightly illuminated hall, and the more Navajo Frank thought about his predicament, the madder he got. Finally, he raised his rifle and fired a bullet through the glass front door of the dance hall. The bullet pierced the heart of pretty Jennie Lawrence, passed through the coat sleeve of her dancing partner, Jimmie Russell of Trinidad, and buried itself in the wall behind the orchestra after passing through the arm of one of the fiddlers. Jennie Lawrence was killed instantly. Navajo Frank disappeared into the darkness, and all efforts to find him were in vain.

The Pecos River country in New Mexico again lured Navajo Frank, and within a short time he was employed as a cowboy by John Chisum, cattle king of the lower Pecos River Valley. The Navajo apparently got into some difficulty with Chisum's Texas cowboys, for he left the ranch hating Texans and determined to kill as many of them as he could. He embarked upon a murdering expedition through the Texas Panhandle, it was said, killing an estimated fifteen to twenty men before being forced to flee west into the mountains of New Mexico.

He turned up next at the Lincoln County mining town of White Oaks, in 1880 or 1881, where he earned his livelihood as a hunter. Late in 1881 or in early 1882 he wandered into Las Vegas, where he was soon accused of shooting and wounding a woman named Lena who resisted his drunken advances. He also was believed to be responsible for the shooting of another woman at Sapello, north of town.

Navajo Frank next settled down at Serafin Polacco's ranch about six miles north of Las Vegas and began operating what he called a burro-trading business, but believed to be a front for a stock-rustling business. He added the name Garcia as an alias.

A big and powerful man, unable to hold his whiskey and described as a demon when drunk, Navajo Frank became an unpopular figure on the Las Vegas scene. On Saturday, June 24, 1882, he spent the day getting liquored up in various Las Vegas saloons. Early in the evening, he climbed on his horse and started north out of town at a fast gallop.

As he approached an open hillside between Douglas Avenue and Main Street, he noticed an elderly couple walking up the hill, their arms laden with groceries. They were Mr. and Mrs. B.H. Hunter, formerly of Topeka, Kansas. Mr. Hunter, a painter, and his wife had been shopping in East Las Vegas and were returning home. Navajo Frank approached the couple from behind at a fast gallop. As he rode his horse between Mr. Hunter and his wife, he dropped his lariat over the elderly man's shoulders, looped the other end of the rope around his saddle horn, and rode on at a full gallop. Hunter was jerked into the air and then dragged about 100 yards behind the horse over rocks and boulders toward the river.

A passing hack driver stopped and fired several shots at Navajo Frank, who immediately drew a knife and cut the rope near the saddle horn. Relieved of the extra weight, he sped off in the distance. Hunter was badly cut and bruised by the ordeal, and it was feared that he would not live, but he managed to recover.

News of the incident spread quickly in Las Vegas, and parties of horsemen were organized to go in pursuit of Navajo Frank. A posse under the leadership of town marshal Harry Franklin headed north on the Sapello road to the Polacco Ranch. Searching ranch buildings, they found

Las Vegas vigilantes dragged Navajo Frank from his jail cell and hanged him from a telegraph pole. (Courtesy Museum of New Mexico, negative 87476)

Navajo Frank sleeping off his drunk in a small *jacal,* or hut. They took him back to town and placed him in the East Las Vegas jail. Sunday afternoon, June 25, Navajo Frank was moved to the more secure jail in West Las Vegas due to growing resentment against him among the townspeople and threats against his life.

Indignation continued to mount during the afternoon and evening, reaching a climax that night when an estimated 300 men gathered at the Gallinas River bridge and decided to take the law into their own hands. The mob marched to the West Las Vegas jail shortly before midnight and battered down the front door. Forcing the guards inside to give up the keys to Navajo Frank's cell, they unlocked and entered it.

"I'll eat up the first man that enters," Navajo Frank shouted as the mob opened the cell door.

The prisoner put up a terrific struggle, and it took some time to overcome him. The rope Navajo Frank had used to drag Hunter behind his horse was produced and placed around his neck, and he was dragged out into the street.

"Hang him where he did the dragging," voices in the crowd shouted.

This site was considered, but instead, the struggling prisoner was led and dragged to a telegraph pole at the Main Street crossing of the railroad. The loose end of the rope was thrown up over a crossarm.

Navajo Frank was allowed two minutes for silent prayer and was then asked if he had anything to say. He said he was innocent, but the crowd didn't believe him, and he was pulled into the air without further struggle.

The Dirty Little Coward

Robert "Bob" Ford was capitalizing on his dubious reputation as the killer of Jesse James when he arrived in Las Vegas in 1884 and entered the saloon business. His partner in the Las Vegas venture was Dick Liddil, who had been a member of the notorious Jesse James gang of bank, train, and stagecoach robbers. Ford had gained national prominence on April 3, 1882, when he shot James to death in the outlaw's home at St. Joseph, Missouri, as his brother, Charles Ford, looked on. The Ford brothers, eager to collect a substantial reward offered for the capture or killing of James, had won the outlaw leader's confidence and were guests in his home, where he had been living incognito, using the name Thomas Howard.

James didn't know it, but Bob Ford and Dick Liddil had killed his favorite cousin, gang member Wood Hite, during an argument over the spoils of a train robbery at the Ford home in Missouri on December 4, 1881. James knew that his cousin was missing, but never learned what had happened to him.

According to the popular story of James' death, he was standing unarmed on a chair dusting and adjusting a picture

Robert "Bob" Ford, killer of Jesse James, served briefly as a Las Vegas policeman. (Courtesy University of Oklahoma Library, Western History Collections, Rose No. 1993)

frame in the front room of his home when Ford walked up close behind him and sent a bullet through the back of his head. The murder weapon was a .44 caliber Smith and Wesson revolver James had given Ford a few days before.

At the inquest, Ford testified that James had stepped down off the chair for a moment to remove his weapons and place them on his bed, he and his brother stepped between him and his weapons, James turned around facing him when he heard his pistol cock, and that he then shot him above the left eye at a distance of about eight feet. He repeated this story for the remainder of his short life.

The twenty-one-year-old Ford considered himself a hero for ridding the country of its most notorious outlaw, in spite of the popular ballad that referred to him as "The dirty little coward, who shot Mr. Howard, and laid poor Jesse in his grave." Ford embarked on a tour of Eastern cities, telling and reenacting his version of his killing of Jesse James to paying audiences. The tour was only moderately successful, however, as most failed to see any heroism in his moment of glory. He often was greeted with hisses and jeers.

Las Vegas, too, was unimpressed with the heroic attitude of Bob Ford, according to Miguel A. Otero, who became acquainted with both Ford and Liddil during their stay in Las Vegas. In his book *My Life on the Frontier,* Otero described Ford as a good-looking young man, rather boyish in appearance, good natured and always endeavoring to make friends. Nevertheless, he said, people shunned him as they might a mad dog. He described Liddil as a rather small man, rough in dress and general appearance, a natural horseman who was much better suited for stable work and attending to horses than in running a saloon business.

James and Liddil became partners in the Bank Saloon in

Dick Liddil, former member of the Jesse James gang, operated saloons in Las Vegas. (Courtesy University of Oklahoma, Western History Collections, Rose No. 1997)

West Las Vegas on Bridge Street between the plaza and the Gallinas River bridge. Ford thought his reputation would attract many customers to the saloon, but in this he was mistaken. The act which he presented, "How I Killed Jesse James," fell flat.

They sold the saloon to Adelido Gonzales, and Liddil found new employment at the recently erected three-story Plaza Hotel on the West Las Vegas plaza. The *Albuquerque Evening Democrat,* which invariably spelled his name Liddel, published this brief item on January 28, 1885: "Dick Liddel, of Missouri train robbery fame, but who has become a good citizen, has leased the bar and billiards tables of the Plaza Hotel in Las Vegas." Less than a month later, on February 26, the Albuquerque newspaper published this item: "Dick Liddel, the ex-train robber and friend of Jesse James, has been arrested in Las Vegas for carrying a pistol. Dick would feel mighty lonely without one."

Liddil didn't stay at the Plaza Hotel very long, for the Democrat reported on March 12 that: "Dick Liddel, the ex-train robber and chum of Jesse James, has retired from the saloon business in Las Vegas." Liddil entered into an agreement with J.W. Lynch of Las Vegas to take a string of Lynch's race horses to Eastern race tracks. Later, he was found dead of natural causes at a race track at Cincinnati, Ohio.

Ford, meanwhile, joined the police force in Las Vegas. The *Albuquerque Democrat* published a brief item on March 27, 1885, saying that Bob Ford had been appointed a policeman in Las Vegas, and repeated the news the next day with some added comment:

> *Las Vegas has morally advanced a notch. It has Bob Ford as a police officer. If any citizen of the meadow town*

hereafter disobeys the law, Bob will bring him to a sense of his duty to good government when said citizen may be hanging a picture.

Citizens of Las Vegas, tired of hearing Ford boast of his killing of Jesse James and of his prowess with a gun, decided that he needed a lesson in humility. The man picked to humiliate him was José Chávez y Chávez, an expert marksman who had fought alongside Billy the Kid in the Lincoln County War of 1878.

Sheriff Cleofas Romero challenged Ford to engage in a shooting match with Chávez y Chávez, each of them to fire at a small target. Reluctantly, Ford agreed to the match. Followed by the sheriff and a large group of citizens, Ford and Chávez y Chávez proceeded to an open space at the outskirts of town. Sheriff Romero stood a small coin on end on a fence post and invited Ford to shoot at it. Ford fired, missing the target by a wide margin. Chávez y Chávez then stepped forward, fired quickly, and hit the coin in the center.

When Ford protested that the match was unfair, Chávez y Chávez challenged him to a duel, suggesting that they stand back to back, walk twenty paces at a given signal, then turn and fire at one another. Ford refused the challenge; thoroughly humiliated, he packed his bags and left town.

His next stop was Cerrillos, a mining town on the railroad south of Santa Fe, where by September he was operating another saloon. The *Albuquerque Democrat* noted that month that Ford was visiting the New Mexico Territorial Fair in Albuquerque from Cerrillos, adding:

After talking a while with Bob, one is impressed with the idea that he is not half as bad as he is painted. On the

The Plaza Hotel on the Las Vegas Plaza. (Courtesy Museum of New Mexico, Jesse Nusbaum photo, negative 6125)

contrary, he is a nice, gentlemanly appearing young man and is far from the desperado-looking person you would expect to meet.

Later, Ford headed north for the mining towns of Colorado, where he opened more saloons. While operating a saloon in Pueblo, he incurred the anger of Edward O'Kelley by accusing him of stealing a diamond ring and later pistol-whipping him. Ford was operating a tent saloon in Creede, Colorado, on June 8, 1892, when O'Kelley walked in the door with a short-barreled shotgun, called "Hello, Bob," and blasted him with slugs. Ford's remains were taken to Richmond, Missouri, for burial.

The Night Riders

I t was nearly midnight on March 11, 1890, when more than 200 armed horseback riders, wearing white hoods pulled down over their faces to conceal their identities, suddenly appeared on the streets of East Las Vegas in a demonstration of strength and determination. Las Gorras Blancas, they were called, The White Caps, a secret and militant organization of rural Hispanic settlers united to protect the common lands of the Las Vegas Land Grant from interlopers.

The horsemen paraded silently through the streets of East Las Vegas, crossed the Gallinas River bridge to West Las Vegas, and circled the plaza. Moving on, they paused silently in front of the home of Sheriff Lorenzo López, then drew up in front of the San Miguel County Courthouse and jail, where they again sat silently for a while before disappearing into the darkness.

This was not the first nocturnal visit of the White Caps to Las Vegas, for smaller numbers of them had staged similar demonstrations there in previous months. This time, however, they scattered circulars in their wake—printed notices explaining their fight against those who were appropriating and fencing tracts of the common lands of the community land grant for their own private use.

Las Gorras Blancas had already demonstrated that they meant business. For a year or more, bands of the hooded night riders had been conducting destructive raids on the properties of those who had purchased or otherwise obtained tracts of the communal lands. Appearing on horseback under cover of darkness, the White Caps tore down miles of wire fencing and fence posts, put the torch to barns and haystacks, and sent livestock scattering. Physical injury seldom was inflicted on the persons of the "land grabbers," as the White Caps called them, although some isolated shootings and killings were blamed on the White Caps.

Confusion as to the status of the Las Vegas Community Land Grant, surveyed in 1860 to measure 496,444.96 acres, led to the White Cap movement and resulting turmoil. As set aside in 1835 under the Mexican government, the lands surrounding Las Vegas, within the grant boundaries, were to be held in joint ownership by the original Las Vegas colonists and their heirs and successors, as undivided community lands open to all for grazing, hunting, and wood gathering. Some officials of the U.S. government were now insisting that the common lands had become a part of the U.S. public domain, eligible for private settlement and development.

These undeveloped grazing lands were coveted by ever-increasing numbers of Anglos, as non-Hispanic newcomers eventually were to become known, as well as by some of the wealthy and influential Hispanic families of the region. Affluent ranchers and land speculators, often with the help of local political leaders and lawyers, began purchasing varying-sized tracts of the common lands from some of the land-grant heirs. They fenced their tracts, moved livestock in, planted crops, diverted water from streams for irrigation purposes, and cut timber in the foothills, often to the detriment of less fortunate Hispanic farmers and ranchers who depended on these lands for their livelihood.

Among these less fortunates was Juan José Herrera, who lived at Ojitos Frios (Cold Springs) about ten miles southwest of Las Vegas. Herrera had served as a captain in the Fourth Infantry of New Mexico Volunteers during the Civil War period in the early 1860s, during which time, according to fellow officer Rafael Chacón, he often "occupied himself in going to dances and wooing the ladies." Following his discharge in May 1862, he apparently kept "wooing the ladies," for a few years later he was forced to flee New Mexico because of a scandal involving a woman.

After living in Colorado and Utah for about two decades, he returned to his San Miguel County homestead to find that a new Anglo neighbor had fenced him off from the common lands. Angrily, he shoved his neighbor into a rain barrel and destroyed his fences.

With the assistance of two younger brothers, Nicanor and Pablo Herrera, Juan José began organizing his neighbors to resist land-grant encroachment, and the White Cap movement was born. The Herrera brothers also became active in the organization of local assemblies—or lodges—of the Knights of Labor, a national union considered rather radical at the time. It was generally believed that the White Caps and the Knights of Labor were one and the same, as White Cap raiding activity increased in the vicinity of each new lodge that was established. Juan José answered that he had never attended a union meeting in which there was any mention of violent acts.

White Cap raiding activity in 1889 was brought to the attention of a San Miguel County grand jury, and indictments were returned against the Herrera brothers and other alleged raiders. The indictments later were dismissed, since no witnesses could be found who could identify any of the defendants as night raiders. The indictments and dismissals both brought noisy but harmless White Cap demonstrations in front of the courthouse in Las Vegas, during which some guns were fired into the air and a few windows broken.

Although there was widespread sympathy for the White Cap movement among the people of Las Vegas, the night riders often were pictured elsewhere as anti-Anglo terrorists and outlaws who were giving New Mexico a bad name. It apparently was in an effort to counter this misconception that the White Caps scattered circulars in Las Vegas on the night of March 11 outlining their positions. The text of the circulars was published in various New Mexico newspapers the next day:

OUR PLATFORM

Not wishing to be misunderstood, we hereby make this our declaration:

Our purpose is to protect the rights and interests of the people in general, and especially those of the helpless classes.

We want the Las Vegas grant settled to the interest of all concerned, and this we hold is the entire community within the grant.

We want no "land grabbers" or obstructionists of any sort to interfere. We will watch them. We are not down on lawyers as a class, but the usual knavery and unfair treatment of the people must be stopped.

Our judiciary hereafter must understand that we will sustain it only when "Justice" is the watchword.

The practice of "double dealing" must cease.

There is a wide difference between New Mexico's "law" and "justice." And justice is God's law, and that we must have at all hazards.

We are down on race issues, and will watch race agitators. We are all human brethren under the same glorious flag.

We favor irrigation enterprises, but will fight any scheme that leads to monopolize the supply of water courses to the detriment of residents living on lands watered by the same streams.

We favor all enterprises, but object to corrupt methods to further the same.

We do not care how rich you get so long as you do it fairly and honestly.

The people are suffering from the effects of partisan "bossism" and these bosses had better quietly hold their peace. The people have been persecuted and hacked about in every which way to satisfy their caprice. If they persist in their usual methods, retribution will be their reward.

We are watching "political informers."

We have no grudge against any person in particular, but we are the enemies of bulldozers and tyrants.

We must have a free ballot and fair count and the will of the majority shall be respected.

Intimidation and the "indictment" plan have no further fears for us. If the old system should continue, death would be a relief to our sufferings. And for our rights our lives are the least we can pledge.

If the fact that we are law abiding citizens is questioned, come out to our houses and see the hunger and desolation we are suffering, and "this" is the result of the deceitful and corrupt methods of "bossism."

Be fair and just and we are with you, do otherwise and take the consequences.

THE WHITE CAPS

1,500 Strong and Gaining Daily

White Cap raids increased in the summer of 1890, the night riders extending their operations onto other Hispanic land grants and into adjoining Santa Fe and Mora counties. One victim was Eugenio Romero, San Miguel County Republican leader, county assessor, and former Las Vegas mayor, who held a contract with the Atchison, Topeka and Santa Fe Railroad to furnish ties for railroad construction. Eugenio and his son, Cleofas, hired men to cut ties from timber south of Las Vegas and haul the ties to the railroad line.

Periodically, bands of White Caps would halt teamsters hauling the ties to the railroad and ask them how much they were being paid. If it was decided they were not being paid enough, they would unload the ties on the ground and chop them up or burn them. One night, the White Caps swept down on Romero's tie stacks alongside the railroad and set them on fire, destroying an estimated 5,000 ties and causing the railroad to cancel the contract. In Santa Fe, an alarmed Gov. L. Bradford Prince considered calling on the territorial militia or U.S. Army troops to patrol the troubled areas.

The Herrera brothers, meanwhile, became active in a new Populist political party that was organized in San Miguel

The Las Vegas Plaza in the 1880s, after the coming of the railroad. (Courtesy Museum of New Mexico, F.E. Evans photo, negative 50798)

County in 1890 to combat the Republican political machine. Called El Partido del Pueblo Unido, or The United Peoples Party, the third party campaigned on anti-landgrabbing and anti-monopoly themes and was successful in electing some of its candidates to office in the 1890 elections.

Elected to the House of Representatives in the New Mexico Territorial Legislature on the Partido ticket was Pablo Herrera, who had served time in prison for killing a man during an argument at Tecolote near his home. After sitting quietly through sessions of the Territorial Assembly in Santa Fe, Herrera decided that he had had enough. At the close of the legislative session, he rose from his seat and delivered this brief address to his colleagues:

> *Gentlemen, I have served several years time in the penitentiary but only 60 days in the Legislature, the present House of Representatives.*
>
> *I have watched the proceedings here carefully.*
>
> *I would like to say that the time I spent in the penitentiary was more enjoyable than the time I spent here.*
>
> *There is more honesty in the halls of the territorial prison than in the halls of the Legislature.*
>
> *I would prefer another term in prison than another election to the House.*

Thus ended Pablo Herrera's brief political career.

In 1891, shortly after his service in the legislature, Herrera was convicted of third-degree murder in connection with the fatal stabbing of Doroteo Sandoval during a melee in Vicente Silva's Imperial saloon on the West Las Vegas plaza, a free-for-all in which Pablo's brothers, Juan José and Nicanor;

215

the slain man's father, Florencio Sandoval; and Deputy Sheriff Billy Green also were involved. A friendly jailer permitted Pablo to escape while he was awaiting sentencing, and a $200 reward later was offered for his arrest.

Herrera was shot to death by a sheriff's posse on a West Las Vegas street on Christmas Eve, 1894. This account of his death was published in *The Evening Citizen* at Albuquerque the same day:

> *East Las Vegas, N.M., Dec. 24—Pablo Herrera, who has been under sentence to the penitentiary for murder for the last two years and who escaped from a deputy and has been coming into town and defying the officers came once too often yesterday. Last night he came in and filled up with whisky, and this morning went out visiting merchants and asking for Christmas gifts, displaying a six-shooter in each place.*
>
> *When court opened this morning, Judge Smith sent for Billy Green and ordered the sheriff and Green to take a posse and go arrest Herrera at all hazards. His friends tried to get him to his horse and Winchester rifle and start him out of town, but the officers caught up with him and headed him off and demanded his surrender. He paid no attention to the order, though called on three times, when the deputies opened fire on him, which he returned. He was shot four times from which he died in a few minutes.*
>
> *A crowd of his friends had gathered in the meantime and attacked the officers, wounding Green quite badly and giving the officers trouble in getting away. Couriers were sent out by Herrera's into the country, and it may be that they will come in and make trouble.*

Other versions of the story were told later, including one that Herrera was shot from ambush on the street without a word of warning.

By the time of Herrera's death, White Cap raids in San Miguel County had ceased, as there were no fences remaining on the common lands and no new ones being built. The land-grant matter was resolved in 1903 when the Town of Las Vegas was given ownership of the disputed lands and a board of trustees was established to administer them. Las Vegas, with the old and new towns having a combined population exceeding 6,000, now ranked alongside Santa Fe and Albuquerque as one of the largest communities in New Mexico.

The Society of Bandits

The lifeless body of Patricio Maes, who had been a wood hauler, was found hanging by the neck from the Gallinas River bridge in Las Vegas very early on the morning of October 22, 1892. The *Las Vegas Optic* speculated that it might prove to be "the first political murder" of the 1892 election campaign in San Miguel County, citing as evidence a notice, signed by the victim, which had been published the day before in the Spanish Republican newspaper, *El Sol de Mayo.* The notice said:

> *Rincón de la Tablason, N.M., October 7th, 1892. Editor of El Sol de Mayo: By these presents, I hereby give notice that from today on, I withdraw from the United Peoples Party, because said party, instead of doing good to the people and complying with its promises, has imposed upon the people prejudicial laws, etc. Seeing that the Republican party is the true party of the people, I adhere myself to said party with all my heart. I subscribe myself, Patricio Maes.*

Maes was survived by his widow and two children at Rincón de la Tablasán, a small settlement a few miles south of Las Vegas. A coroner's jury ruled that Maes "came to his death by hanging at the hands of unknown parties."

The *Optic* wondered what the Las Vegas police were doing when the hanging occurred:

> *The strangest thing of all is that, with the howling mob of shooters upon the street, their brains maddened with the vilest of liquors, the policemen, supposed to be on duty, can say nothing that will in the least tend to unravel this mysterious, damnable murder.*

It was to be many months before the murder mystery was unraveled, many months before it was learned that Patricio Maes had been executed for breaking his vow of silence as a member of a secret crime organization, La Sociedad de Bandidos de Nuevo Mexico (The Society of Bandits of New Mexico).

Confessions of former crime-society members in the spring of 1894 brought to light the sensational story of Vicente Silva, former West Las Vegas tavern owner, and the Society of Bandits he organized from among the desperate men who frequented his saloon and gambling rooms. "They were as tough a bunch of bad men as ever gathered together outside a penal institution," Miguel A. Otero recalled in his book, *My Life on the Frontier.*

In some ways, the Society of Bandits could be called the Hispanic counterpart of the Anglo American Dodge City Gang that had brought so much violence to the Las Vegas scene a decade before. Silva, like Hoodoo Brown before him, managed to maintain an air of respectability in the community, while his followers, like those of Hoodoo Brown, often were known by descriptive nicknames, such as The Shrunken One, The Dull One, The Flat-Nosed One, The Hawk, The Owl, and Frog Legs, and included a few who were members of the local police force. Murder, robbery, thievery, and rustling were rampant in San Miguel County during Silva's reign of terror in the early 1890s, but the citizens did not connect Silva, the businessman, with any of it. His name seldom appeared in Las Vegas newspapers during his lifetime.

Silva's contemporaries described him as a neatly dressed man of medium stature with a red or reddish-brown beard, having more the appearance of an Irishman than a New Mexico Hispanic. His pleasant nature, it was said, concealed a violent temper.

Little is known of Silva's early life. It is believed he was born in 1845 in Bernalillo County, in the outskirts of Albuquerque, and that as a young man he worked as a bartender in a saloon on the Albuquerque plaza.

In Albuquerque, he married Telesfora de Sandoval, described as a plain-looking woman who remained devoted to her husband even though suffering much abuse from him. Leaving Albuquerque, the couple moved north to the mining town of San Pedro, where they operated a grocery store. They moved northeast to Las Vegas in about 1875. Silva opened a saloon, called The Imperial, on the south side of the plaza in West Las Vegas, and as business prospered, he added gambling and meeting rooms. He and his wife occupied living quarters upstairs over the saloon.

In 1885, before Silva embarked on his career in crime, he and his wife adopted a newborn child who had been found abandoned on March 5 of that year in a livery stable owned by John Minner near the Gallinas River bridge. The infant, an Anglo girl, was given the name Emma Silva. There was speculation that the newborn child was the daughter of a young woman from Cleveland, Ohio, who had arrived in Las Vegas with a trained nurse a short time before and had rented a room in a private home. The young Anglo woman, said to have the appearance of a socialite, left Las Vegas at about the time the child was found. Also joining the Silva household over the saloon was Mrs. Silva's brother, Gabriel Sandoval, an intelligent young man in his early twenties whom Silva employed as his business manager.

While Silva maintained a fairly respectable position in the community, his saloon did not, and was carefully avoided by respectable citizens. Open twenty-four hours a day, it attracted men and women of the lowest character and reputation, some of them vagrants who made the saloon their home. Crowded day and night, it was the scene of periodic disturbances, where loud and boisterous language and ribald songs filled the air and drunken brawls often spilled out into the streets.

It was from this saloon element that Silva, motivated by greed, organized his Society of Bandits of New Mexico, consisting of about forty members. In later years, after its demise, the crime organization was popularly referred to as "Vicente Silva and the 40 Thieves."

Members met secretly in rooms at Silva's saloon, and even chose officers, Silva assuming the title "attorney general," apparently so that he could prosecute recalcitrant gang members. The crime society included three members of the West Las Vegas police force: José Chávez y Chávez, the Lincoln County War veteran; Julian Trujillo; and Eugenio Alarid.

Livestock rustling was one of the principal activities of the society. As a gathering place for stolen cattle and horses, Silva purchased a ranch at Monte Largo, a secluded mountain vale south of his former home of San Pedro, more than sixty miles southwest of Las Vegas. Placed in charge of the ranch was Ricardo Romero, an expert horseman and outdoorsman known as El Romo, The Flat-Nosed One, sometimes called The Roman.

Silva's spy and personal messenger was Guadalupe Caballero, known as El Lucheza, The Owl, because it was said he could see better by night than by day. A small, insignificant appearing man, he squatted down against shadowy walls wherever people were around, saying nothing but seeing and hearing everything, and reporting it all to Silva. Another gang member of diminuitive size was Genovevo Avila, a native of Mexico, known in colloquial Spanish as El Cachumeno or El Menguado, The Shrunken One. His motto was "A knife in the back for the tall ones." Antonio José Valdez' peculiar way of walking gave him Spanish nicknames meaning Frog Legs, Monkey Legs, and Pussyfoot. Manuel Gonzales y Baca was called El Mellado, The Dull One or The Toothless One, in colloquial Spanish, and Martín Gonzales y Blea was known as El Moro, The Moor.

Formation of the gang signaled the beginning of a crime wave that shocked Las Vegas and spread into the countryside for miles around. West Las Vegas streets became the scene after dark of shootings, stabbings, rapes, thefts, and property destruction, although not all of this could be attributed directly to the Silva gang.

In 1889, Abraham Abulafie, a Syrian merchant, was found dead in his home, a knife in his back, the victim of a

Bridge Street, Las Vegas, link between the Plaza and the Gallinas River bridge. (Courtesy Museum of New Mexico, negative 66418)

robbery. In 1890, Jacob Stutzman, an elderly and respected tailor, vanished without a trace. Carpio Sais, director and treasurer of the outlying Sabinoso schools, was murdered under the Gallinas River bridge and robbed of the $170 in school funds he was carrying. The dismembered body of another man, never identified, with the initials "J.S." tattooed on his arm, was found in an *arroyo,* or dry gulch, at the outskirts of town.

Among the many ranchers in the region losing livestock to the Silva gang was Capt. José Santos Esquivel, who lived about fifty miles southeast of Las Vegas. In October 1892, when he learned that horses stolen from him had been driven to Silva's secret ranch at Monte Largo, he sent his son, Refugio, and some ranch hands to retrieve them.

Refugio found his way to the secluded ranch, found the stolen horses, now bearing Silva's VS brand, and took the horses to Las Vegas. Boldly entering the Imperial saloon, he asked Silva for an explanation. The embarrassed Silva was unable to give one, but decided that he had a traitor in his midst.

Silva called an emergency meeting of the Society of Bandits on the night of October 21, 1892, at The Imperial. The saloon doors were closed to the public, for the first time ever, at midnight. Society members, entering the back door, convened in their saloon meeting room after midnight where they were told by Silva that they had been betrayed by one of their members. He accused Patricio Maes of telling the Esquivels where their horses could be found. Maes, who denied the accusation, was immediately put to trial by the society, prosecuted by Silva, and defended by gang member Librado

Polanco. While gang members were engaged in a heated argument over the fate of Maes, one of them shouted, "Which of you wants to go to the penitentiary?" The answer was a unanimous, "None of us!"

Maes was led through the dark streets to the Gallinas River bridge, where a rope was fastened around his neck, with the other end tied to a bridge girder. He was thrown over the edge, his dangling body discovered at daybreak.

Capt. Esquivel succeeded in bringing grand-jury indictments against Silva, who fled Las Vegas with several members of his gang. They went into hiding in a cave near the Mora County village of Coyote, now called Rainsville, and in the San Miguel County village of Los Alamos, on the south bank of the Sapello River, about twelve miles northeast of Las Vegas. From these hiding places, Silva and his remaining followers continued their criminal activities.

Mrs. Silva, left destitute by her husband's sudden departure, opened a small restaurant to earn enough to support herself and her adopted daughter, Emma, who was now seven and attending school at a Las Vegas academy. Silva, meanwhile, had taken a mistress called Flor de la Peña, whose real name was said to be Rosario Lucero. He visited her secretly at night in West Las Vegas.

Late on the morning of January 23, 1893, Guadalupe Caballero, The Owl, appeared at the Las Vegas academy in a horse-drawn carriage. On the pretext of taking Emma home for lunch, he drove the girl to Silva at Los Alamos. Silva took her north to Taos and enrolled her in a school there.

Frantically, Mrs. Silva walked the streets of Las Vegas, searching for her missing child—a child she was never to see

The Bank Saloon on Bridge Street, Las Vegas, as it appeared in about 1915.
(Courtesy Museum of New Mexico, negative 49225)

again. The kidnaping of Emma apparently was a ploy to enable Silva to silence both his wife and his brother-in-law, Gabriel Sandoval, before they could tell all they knew about his criminal activities.

Silva's accomplices in a conspiracy to murder his brother-in-law were his three policemen followers, José Chávez y Chávez, Julian Trujillo, and Eugenio Alarid. On the night of February 13, 1893, after leading Sandoval to believe that he was joining them in an effort to rescue the kidnapped Emma from her captors, the trio led the young man through the Catholic cemetery in West Las Vegas to an abandoned mill where Silva was waiting. Upon their arrival at the mill, Silva sprang out of the darkness and stabbed Sandoval to death while the policemen held the victim's arms and beat him over the head with their revolvers. With the help of Guadalupe Caballero, The Owl, they carried Sandoval's body through the darkness to a privy near the back of Silva's saloon and dumped it into the pit, stripping the body of its clothing so that it would slip through the narrow opening.

Mrs. Silva, having lost her child, now searched in vain for her missing brother as well.

Silva, who hoped to flee south to Mexico with Flor de la Peña, needed more money, and he eyed the William Frank mercantile store in Los Alamos as a prime source. With the help of five of his gang, he broke into the store on the night of April 6, 1893, and helped himself. The *Las Vegas Optic* reported the next day:

> *It was one of the boldest and most audacious robberies known for a number of years in this section. It seems that the parties drove up to the store in wagons, and carried off*

large quantities of goods, including several barrels of liq-
uors. They also carried off the safe.

The safe, broken open, was found about a mile from the store in an abandoned house. Missing were all the store's account books and records, the newspaper said, and $25 in cash. The books and records had been burned. The value of the merchandise taken from the store was estimated at about $500. There was no clue as to the identity of the burglars.

About six weeks later, on May 19, 1893, which was prior to the fatal shooting of Pablo Herrera, the former legislator, the following notice was published in the *Las Vegas Optic:*

> *Governor W.T. Thornton has offered the following rewards:*
>
> *For the re-arrest of Pablo Herrera, who was convicted of murder in the third degree at Las Vegas, and who skipped away from the custody of the Sheriff of San Miguel County, $200.*
>
> *For the arrest and conviction of Vicente Silva, now under two indictments for stealing in San Miguel County, $200.*
>
> *For the arrest and conviction of the person or persons who broke open and robbed the store of William Frank, in San Miguel County, $200.*
>
> *For the arrest and conviction of the person or persons guilty of the murder of Jacob Stutzman, at Las Vegas in 1890, $200.*
>
> *For the arrest and conviction of the person or persons guilty of the murder of Abran Abulafie, near Las Vegas, in 1889, $200.*

By coincidence, the newspaper notice was published on the very day that Silva was to meet his death, although that fact was not to be known for some time.

That very morning, the distraught Mrs. Silva had been delivered a message from her husband, saying that he, her brother, Gabriel, and her daughter, Emma, were alive and well, and urging her to pack all her belongings and join them. Silva's message was delivered by gang member Florentino Medrán. He was driving a horse-drawn cart, into which Mrs. Silva was told to load her belongings. Medrán left with her possessions, and Mrs. Silva waited anxiously for the arrival of Genovevo Avila, The Shrunken One, whom she was told would pick her up in a carriage and drive her to her family.

Avila picked her up that evening and drove her northeast out of Las Vegas. Silva met them along the way and accompanied them to Los Alamos, where he ushered his wife into a house. Angrily, he asked her for money, and she gave him all she had—$200. Then he asked for her jewelry, and when she began to protest, he drew a knife and stabbed her to death.

Summoning the five gang members who had been waiting outside, Silva asked them to help wrap his wife's body in a blanket and carry it to a suitable burying place. In the darkness, they carried it to a deep *arroyo* south of the village, threw it to the bottom, and kicked the sandy banks down over it.

Silva's companions were shocked that their leader would kill his wife for her money. He handed each of them ten dollars, and as he did so, they could not help but notice the bulging money belt he wore around his waist. They had just started walking back to the village when Antonio Jose Valdez walked up next to Silva, placed the barrel of his .45 revolver close to Silva's left temple, and pulled the trigger. Silva fell dead to the ground. They divided Silva's money and jewelry among themselves, dragged his body back to the arroyo, threw it in, kicked the banks down over it, and went their separate ways.

It was to be nearly two years before it became generally known that Silva was dead. In the intervening period, however, the violence he had spawned lived on.

Homicides and Hangings

Some members of Vicente Silva's Society of Bandits, in the months following his death, were accused of committing murders that had no apparent connection with the crime society. Among them was Cecilio Lucero, who lived with his wife on a sheep ranch owned by his cousin, Benigno Martínez, about six miles east of Las Vegas.

On the evening of May 25, 1893, for reasons he was never given an opportunity to explain, Lucero shot to death his cousin and a sheepherder, Juan Gallegos, at their sheep camp, then pounded their heads with rocks so that the men were unrecognizable. He tied the ends of ropes around the ankles of the two dead men, fastened the other ends to the necks of two burros, and shooed the burros off, so that the animals dragged the bodies behind them over the rough ground.

Juan Aragón discovered the burros and their macabre burdens the next morning as he proceeded along a wagon road near the murder scene. He hurried to Las Vegas with the news of his ghastly discovery, and officers proceeded immediately to the scene. Sheriff Lorenzo Lopez deputized Manuel

Lucero and Alejo Gonzales to hunt down the murderer, and they returned with Manuel's son, Cecilio. Arrested by his own father, Cecilio suffered further humiliation at a Las Vegas hearing on the afternoon of Monday, May 29, when his wife testified that he had come home shortly after the murder with a haggard appearance and with blood on his shirt and clothing.

The hearing was recessed at 7 P.M. for supper but was never resumed. The reason for this was given in an article in Albuquerque's *The Evening Citizen* on May 31:

> *Cecilio Lucero, the murderer of Benigno Martinez, a sheep owner, and Juan Gallegos, his herder, an account of which was published in The Citizen of last Friday, was lynched by a mob of over 1,000 men, nine-tenths of whom were Spanish-speaking people, at East Las Vegas Monday night at 9:40 o'clock.*

The article went on to say that Lucero had been placed in the East Las Vegas jail during the supper recess of the preliminary hearing, and that a large crowd had gathered in the alley behind the jail and begun an assault on the back door. Officers met the intruders with drawn revolvers, but found themselves confronted by a dozen revolvers and a mob that shouted demands for the jail keys.

There was pandemonium as the crowd rushed into the jail, the newspaper continued, which was followed by shouts of "We've got him!" Lucero, offering no resistance, was taken out into the alley and down Sixth Street to the Board of Trade corner, where a rope was produced and thrown over the crossbar of a telephone pole. Before the rope could be placed around Lucero's neck, however, the crowd decided to move on, as it was "too light and too public at that corner."

They moved west on Douglas Avenue to the G.A.R. Hall, where there were loud cries of "Hang him, hang him," and the rope was produced again, but this place also was not considered suitable. All moved on once again, stopping this time by a telephone pole near the Green, Blackwell and Co. warehouse. The newspaper article continued:

> At 9:42, with one end of the rope around his neck, and the other over the cross-piece of a telephone pole, Cecilio Lucero was given his last opportunity to speak, and his words spoken in Spanish were, "I did not do it. I did not kill them." While being dragged to his doom, he said, "The d———d cowards that killed my cousin! I would like to kill them all!" With his last breath he declared his innocence.

A coroner's jury cut his body down at 10:10 p.m.

Months later, Silva followers came under suspicion in connection with what newspapers called "the vile assassination" of John Daugherty, prominent Mora businessman and rancher and former sheriff of Mora County. Daugherty, who maintained an office in his large Mora home, was reading a newspaper in his office on the evening of December 9, 1893, when he was killed by a bullet fired through a window. The *Evening Citizen* in Albuquerque, which spelled his name "Doherty," had this to say:

> It is learned that Mr. Doherty had just gotten his mail and gone into his office to read his papers when he was fired

*upon and killed. Five of his little children were playing in
his office at the time, and they were so small as not to
comprehend what had been done, but being frightened at
the report of the gun they finally went out and told their
mother about it, who came to the office and found her
husband dead. He was sitting so close to his table that he
fell upon it and remained there, instead of falling to the
floor.*

Daugherty was survived by his wife and twelve children.

Prime suspects in the murder mystery, which was never
solved, included two of Silva's expert livestock rustlers, the
twin brothers Tomás and Juan de Dios Lucero, who were
known to operate in Mora County north of Las Vegas. Many
years later, Tomás Lucero reportedly told a friend, Tom
McGrath of Las Vegas, that he and his brother had persuaded
a disgruntled Daugherty employee named Chávez to fire the
fatal shot and had assisted him in his escape to Colorado.

Hermán (or German) Maestas, another member of the
Silva gang, was hanged in Las Vegas in 1894 for killing a man
he insisted had stolen his wife. The twenty-six-year-old Maestas was secretly married to Rosa Durán by a justice of the
peace in Los Alamos, but he did not register the marriage with
the county clerk as required by law. A short while later, while
serving a sentence in the Las Vegas jail for robbery, he learned
that Rosa, doubting the legality of her marriage to him, had
married Pedro Romero, foreman of a Los Alamos sheep
ranch.

Maestas broke out of jail in March 1894, even though he
had only one more week of his sentence to serve, and with a
friend made his way to Rosa's new home, beat Romero and

tied him to a chair, and took off with Rosa on horseback. She escaped from him, however, and hurried back to her new love. Maestas went after Romero again, this time with Jesús Vialpando, another member of the Silva gang. They hunted him down and shot him to death at a sheep camp.

Maestas was captured a few days later, convicted of murder, and hanged on the stormy afternoon of May 25, 1894 before an audience of 150 men in a small enclosure at the San Miguel County Jail in West Las Vegas. The *Las Vegas Optic* told the story of the hanging that day under a series of headlines that began:

> ### PENALTY PAID!
> *Herman Maestas Expiates His*
> *Crime on the Gallows in*
> *the Las Vegas Jail Yard,*
> *This Afternoon.*
> *The Murderer of Pedro Romero*
> *Sails Off For Eternity As*
> *Coolly as If On a Trip*
> *To Europe.*

Jesús Vialpando, meanwhile, remained at large, having eluded capture and trial for his part in the killing of Romero. In January 1895, Vialpando and two companions, Feliciano Chávez and sixteen-year-old Emilio Ensinias, drove some stolen horses to the mining town of San Pedro and sold them. They were joined in San Pedro by another teenage boy, and the four started back over snow-covered terrain toward San Miguel County.

While crossing the cattle ranch of Lorenzo Martínez in

Santa Fe County, about thirty-five miles southeast of Santa Fe, they killed and butchered a steer belonging to Martínez, built a campfire and cooked the meat at an uninhabited spot known as La Muralla. As they were gathered around the fire eating the meat, Tomás Martínez, a son of the ranch owner, approached them on horseback, followed by his dog, Gallardo. Martínez, who was searching for some missing cattle, dismounted and joined the four at the fire, casting questioning glances at the remains of the steer they had just killed.

Vialpando told his two teenage companions to start down the road, saying that he and Chávez would join them later. Moments later, Vialpando drew his revolver and shot Martínez twice as he stood warming himself by the fire. Chávez then fired at the dog, wounding it slightly, and the dog scampered off toward home. Vialpando and Chávez placed the body of young Martínez in the fire, added more wood, and cremated it.

The wounded dog reached the ranch house at Ojo de la Vaca (Cow Springs) without his master. By whining, barking, and unusual actions, the dog made it clear to the Martínez family that something was wrong and that he wanted to lead them someplace. Maximiliano Martínez, brother of Tomás, called in some ranch hands, and they saddled their horses and followed the dog miles through the snow. The dog led them to the now cold ashes of the campfire.

Looking around and finding nothing unusual except the remains of the butchered steer, they were about to leave when the dog began digging into the ashes and pulled out a burned shoe. Maximiliano recognized the shoe as one belonging to his brother; digging deeper into the ashes, he found human bones.

Martínez and his companions, who picked up and following the trail of four horseback riders through the snow, learned the identities of the four they were following from villagers along the way. They apprehended young Ensinias at Rowe, between Santa Fe and Las Vegas, and the youth readily revealed what had happened at the campfire.

Sheriff's posses found and arrested Vialpando and Chávez at their homes in San Miguel County—Vialpando at Tablazón and Chávez at Las Valles de San Augustín—and the two were taken to Santa Fe to stand trial for murder. Convicted of first-degree murder, they were hanged early on the morning of November 19, 1895, from a scaffold that had been erected at the north edge of the capital city. An estimated crowd of about 3,000, including many women and children, witnessed the double execution.

The Confessions

Vicente Silva and his wife had been mouldering in their makeshift graves for nearly a year when the story of the crime organization he led first became generally known. San Miguel County officials, unable to account for the murders and criminal acts that had swept the county for several years, prevailed upon New Mexico governor William T. Thornton to offer pardons to accomplices and accessories to any of these crimes who would come forward and inform upon their leaders or other participants.

The first to take advantage of the offer was Manuel Gonzales y Baca, El Mellado—The Dull One or The Toothless One—who in the spring of 1894 was jailed in Las Vegas on charges of cattle rustling. Hoping for a pardon before his trial could begin, he offered to tell Lewis C. Fort, the district attorney, all he knew about the crimes to which he had been a participant or witness.

Before a shocked district attorney and other court officials on April 10, 1894, Gonzales y Baca revealed for the first time the story of Vicente Silva and his Society of Bandits of New Mexico, saying that he had served as president of the organization. He told how the society had hanged Patricio Maes from the Gallinas River bridge, and how Gabriel Sandoval had been killed by Silva, his body dumped into the privy pit. If he knew about the deaths of Silva and his wife the year before, however, he said nothing about it, which led the district attorney to believe that Silva was still alive and in hiding.

Two laborers who were sent to the abandoned privy the next day found the remains of Silva's brother-in-law in the pit. The remains were removed and quickly given a decent burial. Arrest warrants were issued for all those Gonzales y Baca had identified as having taken part in the murders of Maes and Sandoval.

The *Albuquerque Weekly Citizen,* on April 25, 1894, published a dispatch from Las Vegas, dated April 18, saying that it had long been known that "a gang of cut throats and horse thieves" had been headquartered in San Miguel County, adding:

> *Vicente Silva, who was probably the boss cut throat, is likely to be apprehended soon. In addition to his nephew, he very likely murdered his wife. He moved from town to a placita some 12 miles north, from which he left at night, and when his rooms were opened it was found that all the furniture was broken, as though a struggle had taken place. It is believed that it was there he murdered his wife, as she has never been seen or heard of since the day before he left there.*

It was, in fact, Silva's brother-in-law, not his nephew, that he had murdered.

The *Las Vegas Optic,* on April 24, said that:

Vicente Silva, the vindictive, blood-thirsty murderer, is said to be running a saloon down in Prescott, Arizona, in company with a fiddler, whose front name is Dionicio, and who accompanied Silva from Los Alamos, where the latter fiend in human form had so brutally stabbed and beaten to death her whom he had sacredly promised at least to honor and protect, probably secreting her lifeless body to a well. Parties down that way have sent to Las Vegas for a photograph of Silva, taken when he wore a full beard.

The Arizona saloon keeper, of course, was not Silva, nor was a man resembling Silva who was arrested later in Colorado and then released.

More than a dozen members of the Silva gang who were found guilty of various charges brought in connection with the deaths of Maes and Sandoval were sentenced to the New Mexico penitentiary by Judge Thomas Smith, a Virginian who had served as a Confederate officer during the Civil War in his native state. The sentences ranged from life imprisonment to three years.

Among those given life sentences were Julián Trujillo and Eugenio Alarid, two of the three policemen-gangsters who had assisted Silva in killing Sandoval and putting his body in the privy. The third, José Chávez y Chávez, escaped arrest by leaving town and going into hiding.

The mystery of Silva's disappearance was solved nearly a year later when Guadalupe Caballero, The Owl, told authorities of the killing of Silva and his wife at Los Alamos. Antonio José Valdez, who had put the bullet in Silva's head, agreed to lead authorities to the burial places of Silva and his wife in the dry *arroyo* bed. A search party left for the scene on the morn-

Sixth Street at Grand Avenue, Las Vegas, in early 1900s. (Courtesy Museum of New Mexico, negative 87473)

ing of March 17, 1895, and after some digging uncovered the remains of the two. The *Albuquerque Citizen* told of the discovery the next day:

> *Las Vegas, March 18—Some excitement was caused here yesterday by the bringing in of the bodies of Vicente Silva and his wife. Silva was the leader of the gang of cut throats who made so much trouble in this county two years ago. He has been badly wanted by the officers since the gang was broken up, and there were rumors that he had been killed and also that he was in Arizona or Colorado.*
>
> *Yesterday Hon. Manuel Baca and a party went out about 12 miles north of here on information obtained from some of the former gang, and found the bodies of both Silva and wife buried near each other. It is understood that Silva was murdered to obtain money supposed to be in his possession and his wife was killed to keep her from informing on the murderers. A coroner's inquest is being held today. It is said that a party who has just been released from the pen threatens to give out some information that implicates some former officials during the investigation.*

The *Albuquerque Daily Democrat* reported on March 20:

> *The coroner's jury are still in session in the Silva case. It is doubtful if the true story of the killing is yet known, except to some few officials, and the stories out are all contradictory. If he retains his position, District Attorney Fort will have all of the San Miguel and Mora county gangs in the penitentiary or hung before he stops.*

Two months later, the fugitive Chávez y Chávez was tracked down and arrested by Socorro County Sheriff Holm O. Bursum at a sheep ranch in the Oscura Mountains in the western part of Socorro County, about 150 miles southwest of Las Vegas, where the former policeman-gangster had been working as a sheepherder and using the name José Gonzales. Returned to Las Vegas, he stood trial in June 1895, was convicted of first-degree murder in connection with the death of Gabriel Sandoval, and ordered by Judge Smith that he be hanged on July 10, 1895. The death sentence was commuted to life imprisonment, however, and Chávez y Chávez later was released from the penitentiary in Santa Fe as a reward for assisting prison guards during a riot. This was not before his suffering the indignity of being returned to Las Vegas with a prison gang to hack out a road in nearby Gallinas Canyon, however.

Emma, the adopted daughter of the Silvas, orphaned by their deaths, was reared by Vicente Silva's mistress, Rosario Lucero (Flor de la Peña), along with her own son, Hilario Lucero, who was believed by many to have been fathered by Silva. Emma Silva was married in Las Vegas in 1904 to Victor Rodriguez, a sawmill worker, and they became the parents of two sons, Estanislado and Epifanio Rodriguez. She suffered fatal burns at her home west of Las Vegas in 1911 when her clothing was ignited by fire.

Few if any of the Silva gang members served their full prison sentences, and most returned home to spend the remainder of their lives as respectable, law-abiding citizens, some living into the 1930s. Silva's killer, Antonio José Valdez, sentenced to prison for three years for cattle theft, later served as town marshal of Wagon Mound, a small town north of Las Vegas at the foot of the natural eminence of the same name.

Chávez y Chávez, as an elderly man in Las Vegas, amazed young admirers with his displays of excellent marksmanship, now shooting at tin cans and such instead of living targets. In relating stories of his adventurous life, he told of his boyhood, herding sheep in the Pecos River Valley near Puerto de Luna, and of his friendship with Billy the Kid. He described his escape with Billy through a hail of bullets from the burning Alexander McSween home in Lincoln during the Lincoln County War, and his service with the Lincoln County Mounted Riflemen, a militia unit organized by Gov. Lew Wallace in 1878 in an effort to bring law and order to the embattled region.

Chávez y Chávez also claimed that it was he, and not Billy the Kid, who had shot down Lincoln County Sheriff William Brady and his deputy, George Hindman, on a Lincoln street during the civil conflict. It was for his part in the ambush slaying of Brady that the Kid had been convicted of murder and sentenced to be hanged. "Billy the Kid got the blame, but I'm the one who shot them," Chávez y Chávez told friends.

In 1896, Manuel C. de Baca, a Las Vegas newspaperman and law clerk who had heard the confessions of members of the Silva gang and who had helped locate the bodies of Silva and his wife, published a highly moralistic and melodramatic book entitled *Vicente Silva and his 40 Bandits.* Published first in a Spanish-language edition, it has been reprinted over the years in both Spanish and English versions, and is the basic source for all that is known of the Society of Bandits of New Mexico.

End of an Era

After a period of relative quiet, sounds of gunfire once again echoed through the streets of Las Vegas in the summer of 1915 in daily scenes reminiscent of the community's violent past. Masked bandits held up and robbed stagecoaches at Gallinas River crossings, lawmen and outlaws fought pitched battles, and a young man in a white hat came riding to the rescue with blazing six-shooters. By this time, however, it was all make-believe.

Motion-picture cameras caught the action in black and white as Las Vegas residents, firing blank cartridges, earned twenty-five cents a day as movie extras, acting out episodes recalling the Western frontier. The young hero in the white hat was Tom Mix, just emerging as America's favorite cowboy screen star. Las Vegas' brief career as an early motion-picture center followed a series of events that had brought the community to national attention on several occasions since just before the turn of the century.

In the summer of 1899, Col. Theodore Roosevelt arrived in town amid much fanfare to attend the first annual reunion of his famed Rough Riders, veterans of the Spanish American

Col. Theodore Roosevelt and friends at the first Rough Riders Reunion, Las Vegas, in 1899. (Courtesy Museum of New Mexico, negative 14292)

War who had served with the First Regiment of U.S. Volunteer Cavalry, a regiment that drew more than one-third of its members from New Mexico. Between parades, speeches, band concerts, rodeo events, and fireworks displays, Roosevelt let it be known for the first time that he was available for the presidency of the United States.

In 1912, the year New Mexico ceased to be a territory of the United States and was admitted to the Union as the forty-seventh state, Las Vegas was chosen as the site of the world heavyweight title match between Jack Johnson, first black prizefighter to hold the title, and "white hope" challenger Jim Flynn, "The Fighting Fireman" from Pueblo, Colorado.

Both the champion and the challenger arrived in Las Vegas in May of that year to begin training for the fight, to be held in a makeshift outdoor arena in East Las Vegas on the Fourth of July. Johnson, who scandalized some Las Vegas residents by arriving with his wife, an attractive white woman, rented a house near the West Las Vegas plaza, while Flynn set up his training quarters at the elaborate Montezuma Hotel at the hot springs north of town.

Las Vegas took on a holiday atmosphere as the day of the title fight approached. Special Santa Fe Railway "fight trains" arrived periodically for several days preceding the fight, bringing fight fans from various New Mexico cities and towns and points outside the state. Automobiles, carrying other fight fans, converged on the town from all directions, and one old prospector even arrived with a dog team.

The streets were jammed with people. Hotels put up emergency lunch counters to take care of the overflow, and private citizens set up lunch counters in their yards and invited visitors to sleep on cots in their homes when hotel accommodations were exhausted.

Both prizefighters were confident of victory on the eve of the title fight. Flynn, interviewed at his training camp, told reporters: "I'm going to be champion tomorrow. I'm going to celebrate the Fourth of July. Johnson can't beat me—he knows it."

Johnson told reporters: "I'm going to carry the fight to Flynn and keep carrying it. I'm in a hurry to get back to Chicago, and I won't waste any time fooling around once I get started."

A disappointing crowd of some 3,000 spectators, including many who sneaked under the canvas walls of the outdoor arena without tickets, was on hand on the afternoon of July 4 for the bout, scheduled for forty-five rounds. Telephone and telegraph facilities had been installed in the arena to relay results of the fight to the outside world.

The title fight got under way at 2:49 P.M., and it was apparent from the beginning that Johnson would have no trouble with his Colorado challenger. Flynn's face was cut and bloody by the end of the third unexciting round, even though no serious blow had been struck by either fighter.

In the fourth round, Johnson kept patting his unprotected stomach and inviting Flynn to hit it, causing much laughter among the spectators. The champion was nonchalant during the fifth round, spending part of the time looking at the spectators and talking to his wife, who was seated at ringside, complaining that he couldn't fight while Flynn kept holding him in a clinch. In the sixth round, Flynn began butting Johnson with his head. For this he was reprimanded by the referee, Edward Smith of Chicago. During the slow-moving seventh

Heavyweight champion Jack Johnson and his wife at Las Vegas in 1912 for his title bout with Jim Flynn. (Courtesy Museum of New Mexico, negative 87470)

round, a spectator shouted to the champion, asking him why he didn't end the fight. "Wait a minute," Johnson replied. The champion jabbed Flynn with a series of sharp upper-cuts during the eighth round, while the challenger kept butting Johnson with his head.

At the beginning of the ninth round, Johnson held Flynn at arm's length to protect himself from the constant head butting. Flynn managed to get in close to the champion, then suddenly jumped about a foot upwards, striking Johnson's jaw with the top of his head. At this moment, Capt. Fred Fornoff of the New Mexico Mounted Police, who had been seated at ringside at the request of New Mexico Gov. William C. McDonald, vaulted into the ring and stopped the fight. Referee Smith immediately gave the decision to Johnson. The state police captain, criticized by some for stopping the fight, said he brought the bout to an end because "it was no longer a skillful boxing exhibition, but a test of brute strength and roughbone methods."

Johnson left Las Vegas the next day with $36,000, consisting of his $30,000 guarantee, $1,000 for expenses, and $5,000 he had won betting on himself.

A San Francisco motion-picture company filmed the fight, and released a condensed version showing parts of each round. Romaine Fielding, the flamboyant manager, director, actor, and writer for the Western division of the Lubin Film Co. of Philadelphia, arrived in Las Vegas with his troupe in August of 1913 and announced that he planned to settle there permanently and film motion pictures in the area. Fielding was lured to the region by its wide variety of scenery, ranging from rugged mountains to rolling meadows and broad plains, and its old buildings that provided a Mexican atmosphere.

Fielding rented a residence on Gallinas Street in East Las Vegas for use as a studio, but soon abandoned it to lease the entire Plaza Hotel on the West Las Vegas plaza, changing the name of the three-story structure to Hotel Romaine in the process. He produced several motion pictures in and about Las Vegas in following months, including one called *The Rattlesnake,* a story of a love triangle set in Mexico.

Fielding's most ambitious effort, however, was *The Golden God,* a five-reel action film set in the future, concerning a labor revolution against consolidated industries. Several thousand Las Vegas residents were employed as extras to stage battle scenes and cavalry and artillery maneuvers. For this movie Fielding brought an airplane to Las Vegas—the first one seen in the community—from which smoke bombs were dropped on battle scenes. Winter snows and icy winds apparently changed Fielding's mind about staying in Las Vegas, however, for in December he suddenly announced that he was moving his company to the warmer climate of the Texas Gulf Coast.

Las Vegas, now considering itself the "cowboy capital" of New Mexico because of the many cattle ranches in the area, began staging an annual Cowboys Reunion in the summer of 1915. During the event cowboys were invited to compete in riding, roping, and other rodeo events and to attend dances and other festivities.

Among invited guests at the first annual Cowboys Reunion that July were Tom Mix and his wife, actress Virginia Forde. After filming some of the cowboy contestants in action, Mix decided to stay in Las Vegas to continue his career of starring in cowboy movies. The Selig-Polyscope Co. was already in the vicinity, filming the serial *The Hazards of Helen,* which starred Helen Holmes.

Cowboy star Tom Mix and his leading lady, Virginia Forde, in a scene from "Local Color," filmed in Las Vegas in 1915. (Courtesy New Mexico State Records Center, Movie Stills Collection No. 39344)

Mix took over Fielding's original studio on Gallinas Street, obtained authentic Western props and paraphernalia including old stagecoaches, hired Las Vegas residents as extras, and for the next year filmed cowboy Westerns including *Never Again, Local Color, The Rancher's Daughter,* and *The Country Drugstore.* Las Vegas elders watched with silent amusement as stagecoaches once again rolled through streets now served by electric streetcars and members of the younger generation reenacted action scenes of the Western frontier that were all too vivid in their memories. They had seen it all—the violence and trauma of life in the frontier West—and now they were seeing it again, staged this time for the entertainment of paying customers in comfortable movie houses over the nation.

Those who had passed their eightieth birthdays were older than Las Vegas itself, their long lives extending back to the time when a small group of Mexican farmers trudged into hostile Indian country to stake out a tiny settlement they called Nuestra Señora de los Dolores de Las Vegas, Our Lady of Sorrows of the Meadows. From ox cart to airplane, they had seen it all.

EPILOGUE

Las Vegas today is a New Mexico city of some 14,000 inhabitants, its very existence obscured by its younger but much larger and more glamorous namesake in Nevada. Still the seat of San Miguel County, Las Vegas leads a fairly quiet existence as a business and shopping center for a sparsely populated region of farmers and ranchers in northeastern New Mexico. Of major industries it has none, the largest employers being New Mexico Highlands University and the New Mexico Mental Hospital.

West Las Vegas, the original 1835 settlement, and East Las Vegas, created by the coming of the railroad in 1879, were consolidated under a single city government in 1970 after existing as adjoining but separate political entities for nearly a century. The west and east sides of the once-divided community are referred to locally as Old Town and New Town.

Evidences of the past abound in and about Las Vegas, a city with more than 900 buildings on the National Register of Historic Places, enabling the community to retain much of its frontier atmosphere and spirit. These historic landmarks represent all phases of Las Vegas history, ranging from adobe structures of the Mexican period to substantial and ornate buildings and residences of brick or stone of the Victorian era. After a long period of neglect and decay, older sections of the city are being revitalized through a community effort to preserve and restore historic landmarks and make them suitable for modern enterprises.

The Old Town plaza, heart of the original settlement, is now a grassy and tree-shaded park with walkways and benches, a city block surrounded by old business buildings. A roofed bandstand, or gazebo, stands in the center of the park near the site of the "hanging windmill." Facing the park on the north is the one-story building on which Gen. Stephen Watts Kearny stood in 1846 when he proclaimed to the assembled populace below that he was taking possession of New Mexico on behalf of the United States. Just up the street is the recently renovated and refurbished Plaza Hotel, dating from the early 1880s. Across the park from the three-story hotel is the building that once housed Vicente Silva's Imperial Saloon and gambling rooms.

Most of New Town's earliest landmarks along the railroad, those associated with the Dodge City Gang, were destroyed a series of fires in 1881 and 1882, including the establishments of Doc Holliday and Monte Verde on Centre (or Center) Sreet, now Lincoln Street. But this, the downtown business district of Las Vegas, includes a number of century-old buildings.

The *Las Vegas Optic,* which arrived in East Las Vegas in 1879 with the railroad and recorded for posterity the stories of frontier life in the region, continues to this day as the only daily newspaper in Las Vegas and the surrounding area.

The castle-like Montezuma Hotel at the hot springs north of town, one of a succession of elaborate hotels built at the popular resort, is now a part of the 110-acre campus of the Armand Hammer United World College, an international high school.

North and south of Las Vegas, you can still see traces of the historic Santa Fe Trail, paralleling Interstate 25 and the Santa Fe Railway tracks at varying distances—weather-eroded ruts across the meadowlands left by thousands of wagon wheels that stopped turning more than a century ago.

The nomadic Jicarilla Apache and Ute Indians, who once considered this a part of their homeland, were eventually settled on reservations along the New Mexico-Colorado border more than 100 miles northwest of Las Vegas, where their descendants live today.

Fort Union, abandoned in 1891 after decades of service as a guardian of the Santa Fe Trail, stands today as an impressive array of roofless buildings in a broad valley northeast of Las Vegas, the extensive ruins preserved and maintained as a national monument.

Los Alamos, Vicente Silva's hideout near Las Vegas, not to be confused with the "atomic city" of Los Alamos established near Santa Fe during the early 1940s, has ceased to be a village, and the few buildings now serve as a ranch headquarters.

Mora, resurrected after being destroyed by U.S. troops in 1847, clings to a precarious existence north of Las Vegas as a small county seat in a scenic but economically depressed region. Mills that once ground grain for Fort Union still stand there and in the vicinity, their wheels now motionless.

Southwest of Las Vegas, the once populous town of San

Miguel del Bado, from which the original Las Vegas colonists came, has faded into obscurity a few miles off Interstate 25 as a small cluster of old buildings facing an early nineteenth-century church at what once was the fording place of the Pecos River.

SOURCES AND ACKNOWLEDGMENTS

As is evident from the text, much of the material in this book was drawn from the pages of frontier newspapers, particularly the *Las Vegas Optic* and *Las Vegas Gazette,* and including articles from these newspapers that were reprinted in other newspapers. Many of the episodes described are based on my New Mexico history columns, originally titled "Off the Beaten Path," which have been published in *The Albuquerque Tribune* continuously since 1953.

Lauro E. Flores of Albuquerque, a Las Vegas pioneer, who as a young man was personally acquainted with eight veterans of the Vicente Silva gang, furnished some of his recollections. Andy Gregg of Albuquerque provided notes on his newspaper research into activities of the Dodge City Gang, as well as some old photographs.

Marc Simmons of Cerrillos, New Mexico, authority on the Santa Fe Trail, and Charles and Jacqueline Meketa of Albuquerque, authorities on New Mexico military history, assisted in clearing up some obscure points. Diana Stein of Las Vegas furnished material on Las Vegas landmarks.

Various issues of the *New Mexico Historical Review,* quarterly publication of the University of New Mexico, and *El Palacio,* quarterly publication of the Museum of New Mexico, were consulted, as well as the Special Centennial Edition of the *Las Vegas Optic* published on July 27, 1979.

Files of early newspapers, original or on microfilm, were examined courtesy the University of New Mexico Library, the Museum of New Mexico Historical Library, and the Albuquerque Publishing Company.

Mickie Herbert Griggs of Albuquerque was of great assistance in typing the early phases of the manuscript.

BIBLIOGRAPHY

Abel, A.H., ed. *The Official Correspondence of James S. Calhoun.* Washington: Government Printing Office, 1915.

Arrellano, Anselmo F., and Vigil, Julian J. *Las Vegas Grandes on the Gallinas.* Las Vegas: Editorial Telerana, 1985.

Barry, Louise. *The Beginning of the West.* Topeka: Kansas State Historical Society, 1972.

Bartholomew, Ed. *Wyatt Earp.* 2 vols. Toyahvale: Frontier Book Company, 1964.

Briggs, Charles L., and Van Ness, John R., eds. *Land, Water and Culture.* Albuquerque: University of New Mexico Press, 1987.

C de Baca, Manuel. *Vicente Silva and his 40 Bandits.* Washington, D.C.: Edward McClean, 1947.

Callon, Milton W. *Las Vegas, New Mexico—The Town that Wouldn't Gamble.* Las Vegas: Las Vegas Publishing Company, 1962.

Cooke, Philip St. George. *The Conquest of New Mexico and California.* Reprint. Albuquerque: Horn and Wallace, 1964.

Drago, Harry Sinclair. *Notorious Ladies of the Frontier.* New York: Dodd, Mead and Company, 1969.

Garrett, Pat F. *The Authentic Life of Billy the Kid.* Reprint. Albuquerque: Horn and Wallace, 1964.

Gregg, Josiah. *Commerce of the Prairies.* Reprint. Norman: University of Oklahoma, 1954.

Hammond, George P. *Alexander Barclay, Mountain Man.* Denver: Old West Publishing Company, 1976.

Hoyt, Henry F. *A Frontier Doctor.* New York: Houghton Mifflin Company, 1929.

Jahns, Pat. *The Frontier World of Doc Holliday.* New York: Hastings House, 1957.

Keleher, W.A. *Turmoil in New Mexico.* Santa Fe: Rydal Press, 1952.

McGrath, Tom. *Vicente Silva and his 40 Thieves.* Las Vegas: 1960.

Meketa, Jacqueline D. *Legacy of Honor.* Albuquerque: University of New Mexico Press, 1986.

Miller, Nyle H., and Snell, Joseph W. *Great Gunfighters of the Kansas Cowtowns, 1867–1886.* Lincoln: University of Nebraska Press, 1963.

Otero, Miguel Antonio. *My Life on the Frontier.* 2 vols. Reprint. Albuquerque: University of New Mexico Press, 1987. New York: Press of the Pioneers, 1935.

Perrigo, Lynn. *Gateway to Glorieta, A History of Las Vegas, New Mexico.* Boulder: Pruett Publishing Company, 1982.

Poldervaart, Arie W. *Black-Robed Justice.* Santa Fe: Historical Society of New Mexico, 1948.

Rickards, Colin. *Mysterious Dave Mather.* Santa Fe: Press of the Territorian, 1968.

Sabin, Edwin L. *Kit Carson Days.* New York: Press of the Pioneers, 1935.

Stanley, F. *Dave Rudabaugh, Border Ruffian.* Denver: World Press, 1961.

Stratton, Porter A. *The Territorial Press of New Mexico.* Albuquerque: University of New Mexico Press, 1969.

Tiller, Veronica E. Velarde. *The Jicarilla Apache Tribe.* Lincoln: University of Nebraska Press, 1983.

Twitchell, Ralph Emerson. *The History of the Military Occupation of New Mexico.* Reprint. Chicago: Rio Grande Press, 1963.

———. *The Leading Facts of New Mexico History,* Vol. 4. Cedar Rapids: The Torch Press, 1917.

INDEX